Transformations of the Radical Left in Southern Europe

Political parties are alleged to be turning their backs to civil society; they are said to discourage the active participation of their members and to distance themselves from the privileged relations to affiliated social organisations they once prized. Instead, parties are broadly believed to be directing their efforts towards capturing government office and the resources that come with it, neglecting linkage to their social roots. *Transformations of the Radical Left in Southern Europe* questions this widely shared view. Exploring the social linkage strategies of the most relevant radical left parties in Portugal, Spain, Italy, Greece and Cyprus in depth, this book demonstrates that the members of the European radical left party family continue to prioritise social linkage, despite their increasingly office-seeking orientation. Between the fall of the Berlin Wall in 1989, and the current economic crisis, they have been tirelessly experimenting with diverse new forms of party organisation that have enabled them to return to their social roots. The main lesson drawn from the studies in this book is that party ideology and a party's position in the national political arena go a long way towards explaining the extent to which political parties prioritise social linkage.

This book was published as a special issue of *South European Society and Politics.*

Myrto Tsakatika is Senior Lecturer at the School of Social and Political Sciences, University of Glasgow, UK. Her main fields of research are European Union governance, South European politics and radical left parties. Her recent publications appear in the *Journal of Common Market Studies*, the *Journal of European Public Policy*, *Europe-Asia Studies* and *South European Society and Politics.*

Marco Lisi is Assistant Professor at the Department of Political Studies, Nova University of Lisbon, Portugal. His research and publications have analysed political parties and voting behaviour, especially in Southern Europe. He has published several articles in international journals such as *West European Politics*, *South European Society and Politics* and *Representation*.

South European Society and Politics series

Series editors:

Susannah Verney, University of Athens, Greece

Anna Bosco, University of Trieste, Italy

The parallel regime transitions of the 1970s, when Southern Europe was the vanguard of the 'third wave' of democratisation, the impact of EU membership and Europeanisation and more recently, the region's central role in the eurozone crisis have all made Southern Europe a distinctive area of interest for social science scholars. The *South European Society and Politics* book series promotes new empirical research into the domestic politics and society of South European states. The series, open to a broad range of social science approaches, offers comparative thematic volumes covering the region as a whole and on occasion, innovative single-country studies. Its geographical scope includes both 'old' and 'new' Southern Europe, defined as Italy, Greece, Portugal, Spain, Cyprus, Malta and Turkey.

Voters and Parties in the Spanish Political Space
Edited by Ignacio Sánchez-Cuenca and Elias Dinas

Elections in Hard Times: Southern Europe 2010-11
Edited by Anna Bosco and Susannah Verney

Transformations of the Radical Left in Southern Europe
Bringing Society Back In?
Edited by Myrto Tsakatika and Marco Lisi

Previously published in the journal South European Society and Politics

Europeanization and the Southern Periphery
Edited by Kevin Featherstone and George Kazamias

Who Governs Southern Europe?
Edited by Pedro Tavares de Almeida, Nancy Bermeo and Antonio Costa Pinto

Spain and Portugal in the European Union
The First Fifteen Years
Edited by Paul Christopher Manuel and Sebastian Royo

Mobilising Politics and Society?
The EU Convention's Impact on Southern Europe
Edited by Sonia Lucarelli and Claudio Radaelli

Reinventing Democracy
Grassroots Movements in Portugal
Edited by João Arriscado Nunes and Boaventura de Sousa Santos

When Greeks think about Turks
The View from Anthropology
Edited by Dimitrios Theodossopoulos

Party Change in Southern Europe
Edited by Anna Bosco and Leonardo Morlino

The South European Right in the 21st Century
Italy, France and Spain
Edited by Jocelyn A. J. Evans

Spain's 'Second Transition'?
The Socialist government of Jose Luis Rodriguez Zapatero
Edited by Bonnie N. Field

Dealing with the Legacy of Authoritarianism
The "Politics of the Past" in Southern European Democracies
Edited by Antonio Costa Pinto and Leonardo Morlino

Perspectives of National Elites on European Citizenship
A South European View
Edited by Nicolò Conti, Maurizio Cotta and Pedro Tavares de Almeida

Euroscepticism in Southern Europe
A Diachronic Perspective
Edited by Susannah Verney

Turkey and the EU: Accession and Reform
Edited by Gamze Avci and Ali Çarkoğlu

Transformations of the Radical Left in Southern Europe

Bringing Society Back In?

Edited by

Myrto Tsakatika and Marco Lisi

Routledge
Taylor & Francis Group
LONDON AND NEW YORK

First published 2014
by Routledge
2 Park Square, Milton Park, Abingdon, Oxon, OX14 4RN

Simultaneously published in the USA and Canada
by Routledge
711 Third Avenue, New York, NY 10017

Routledge is an imprint of the Taylor & Francis Group, an informa business

British Library Cataloguing in Publication Data
A catalogue record for this book is available from the British Library

ISBN 13: 978-0-415-86980-5

Typeset in Goudy
by Taylor & Francis Books

Publisher's Note
The publisher accepts responsibility for any inconsistencies that may have arisen during the conversion of this book from journal articles to book chapters, namely the possible inclusion of journal terminology.

Disclaimer
Every effort has been made to contact copyright holders for their permission to reprint material in this book. The publishers would be grateful to hear from any copyright holder who is not here acknowledged and will undertake to rectify any errors or omissions in future editions of this book.

Contents

Citation Information

The chapters in this book were originally published in the *South European Society and Politics*, volume 18, issue 1 (March, 2013). When citing this material, please use the original page numbering for each article, as follows:

Chapter 1
'Zippin' up My Boots, Goin' Back to My Roots': Radical Left Parties in Southern Europe
Myrto Tsakatika and Marco Lisi
South European Society and Politics, volume 18, issue 1 (March, 2013)
pp. 1–20

Chapter 2
Rediscovering Civil Society? Renewal and Continuity in the Portuguese Radical Left
Marco Lisi
South European Society and Politics, volume 18, issue 1 (March, 2013)
pp. 21–40

Chapter 3
Impulse and Decadence of Linkage Processes: Evidence from the Spanish Radical Left
Luis Ramiro and Tània Verge
South European Society and Politics, volume 18, issue 1 (March, 2013)
pp. 41–60

Chapter 4
Renewal and Tradition: Comparing Italian Radical Left Parties through their Middle-Level Elites
Paola Bordandini
South European Society and Politics, volume 18, issue 1 (March, 2013)
pp. 61–80

Chapter 5
The Radical Left's Turn towards Civil Society in Greece: One Strategy, Two Paths
Myrto Tsakatika and Costas Eleftheriou

South European Society and Politics, volume 18, issue 1 (March, 2013)
pp. 81–100

Chapter 6
A Society within Society: Linkage in the Case of the Cypriot Communist Party
Giorgos Charalambous and Christophoros Christophorou
South European Society and Politics, volume 18, issue 1 (March, 2013)
pp. 101–119

Please direct any queries you may have about the citations to clsuk.permissions@cengage.com

'Zippin' up My Boots, Goin' Back to My Roots': Radical Left Parties in Southern Europe

Myrto Tsakatika and Marco Lisi

Radical left parties actively encourage the participation of their members in internal decision-making and insist on promoting organised links to trade unions and social movements. As a party family, they deviate from what is considered to be the trend in which Western political parties have turned their backs on their social roots. Drawing on the experience of South European radical left parties from the fall of the Berlin Wall until the recent financial crisis, we argue that ideology, electoral incentives, party competition and external events explain the radical left's pronounced emphasis on linkage, while organisational trajectory explains variation within the party family in terms of the linkage strategies pursued.

According to Katz and Mair's (1995) influential 'cartel party' thesis, political parties are increasingly orienting their actions towards occupying the state while disengaging from their social roots. It is said that there is no longer a strong incentive for parties to encourage members to take an active role, since the functions they once performed such as party funding and labour-intensive campaigning are now being replaced by state funding and mass media campaigns, respectively. It is likewise argued that parties are confronted with incentives to distance themselves from organisations of civil society, because their appeal is increasingly directed beyond their particular social constituency. Strong and exclusive party links to a small, well-defined range of interest groups carry the risk of alienating other civil society organisations and place excessive constraints on the range of policies that parties can pursue (Kirchheimer 1966). Declining membership figures (Van Biezen, Mair & Poguntke 2011) and an overall trend of loosening and pluralisation of party–civil-society ties (Allern & Bale 2012a) are thought to confirm these arguments.

A number of scholars have challenged or qualified the mainstream view that parties are turning their backs on their social roots (Yishai 2001; Caul Kittilson & Scarrow 2003; Allern & Bale 2012b). They have argued that political parties continue to pursue linkage because their electoral stability (Poguntke 2002; Scarrow 2009), legitimacy (Warner 2000, p. 164; Allern 2010) and even—to a certain extent—funding (Pedersen et al. 2004), continue to depend on it. Their research has shown that parties have tended to encourage the active involvement of members (and in some cases sympathisers) by strengthening their rights in candidate and leadership selection (Caul Kittilson & Scarrow 2003; Hazan & Rahat 2010; Cross & Blais 2012) and party policy-making (Gauja 2009). It has also demonstrated that parties have maintained formal ties (Aarts 1995; Poguntke 2002) and, most importantly, enhanced their informal interactions with civil society groups through joint committee meetings, common campaigns and invitations to civil society organisations, whose purpose is to engage them in drawing up party manifestos and key decision-making (Thomas 2001; Poguntke 2006; Allern 2010). It has also been found that parties try to establish new links to social organisations that emerge as a result of social change (Yishai 2001), to create new ancillary structures, such as youth and women's organisations (Poguntke 2002) and to take the initiative to build new external civic organisations (Kitschelt 2006; Verge 2012) in order to target new supporters.

This special issue aims to add to the above voices by examining the linkage strategies of the European radical left party family. Radical left parties have recovered from the collapse of communism (March 2011, p. 1). They have not only remained politically and electorally relevant in European party systems, but also been essential partners in government coalitions (Bale & Dunphy 2011). Contrary to what might be expected on the basis of Katz and Mair's thesis and despite an increasingly common office-seeking orientation, not only have the parties of the European radical left remained committed to their social roots, but there are valid indications that they have prioritised linkage and introduced significant organisational innovations *in order* to pursue the strengthening of ties to their social roots more effectively. Comparative study of radical left parties' distinctive efforts to pursue linkage, as advanced in this special issue, allows us to explore the factors that make it more likely for political parties to prioritise linkage, and consequently to revisit an important aspect of the contemporary theory of party change. We also aim to make a significant contribution to the emerging new research agenda on radical left parties, particularly to the study of their organisational development, social linkages and mobilisation strategy (Bosco 2000; March & Mudde 2005; Della Porta 2007; March 2011; De Waele & Seiler 2012).

The article proceeds as follows. In the next section we present the broad parameters of the research design adopted by the works in this special issue. Drawing on data from the case studies examined in this volume, the third section identifies the instances in which South European radical left parties have launched linkage strategies over the last two decades and sets out to explain why they did so. The fourth section discusses the main findings in terms of how the parties examined have pursued linkage and what kinds of organisational innovations they have introduced to that effect, focusing on the differences between them. The fifth section examines the relationship between the radical left and civil society during the economic crisis. A final section concludes with a summary and suggestions for further research.

Linkage in a Crisis Zone

This special issue brings forth original data on the efforts made to strengthen linkages to their social roots since the fall of the Berlin Wall by all relevant radical left parties in Portugal—Partido Comunista Português (Portuguese Communist Party, PCP) and Bloco de Esquerda (Left Bloc, BE), Spain—Izquierda Unida (United Left, IU), Italy—Federazione della Sinistra (Left Federation, FDS) and Sinistra Ecologia e Libertà (Left Ecology and Freedom, SEL), Greece—Κομμουνιστικό Κόμμα Ελλάδας (Communist Party of Greece, KKE) and Συνασπισμός της Αριστεράς της Οικολογίας και των Κοινωνικών Κινημάτων (Coalition of the Left, Ecology and Social Movements, SYN)/Συνασπισμός Ριζοσπαστικής Αριστεράς (Coalition of the Radical Left, SYRIZA)[1] and the Republic of Cyprus—Ανορθωτικό Κόμμα Εργαζομένου Λαού (Progressive Party of the Working People, AKEL). Given that the FDS and SEL are very recent formations that have yet to compete in national elections, in this article we complement our analysis of the Italian case with data from secondary sources regarding the linkages to civil society of the Partito della Rifondazione Comunista (Communist Refoundation Party, PRC) and the Partito dei Comunisti Italiani (Party of Italian Communists, PdCI), both relevant parties of the radical left throughout most of the 1990s and 2000s.

The studies in this special issue focus on 'participatory' linkage, namely relations between the party leadership and party members (as well as sympathisers in some cases), and 'environmental' linkage, i.e. relations between the party and organised groups in civil society. Kay Lawson conceptualised political parties as agencies that forge links between citizens and policy-makers, introducing the notion of 'participatory' linkage (Lawson 1980). Parties use participatory linkages to mobilise and involve their members in the political process by channelling the expression and representation of their preferences. Building on Lawson's work, Schwartz looks at parties as 'multi-unit' organisations that are simultaneously engaged in building and maintaining relations among the party subunits and between the party and its external environment (Schwartz 2005). While Lawson's 'participatory linkage' can be conceptualised as one of the most important forms of relations between the party's subunits, what Schwartz calls 'environmental linkage' concerns the relation between the party and groups active in its social environment. Parties, she notes, 'normally seek to mobilise supporters in terms of demographic or other characteristics, not as indistinguishable voters' (Schwartz 2005, pp. 38–39). Environmental linkage buttresses one of the essential functions played by political parties, that is, articulating and aggregating interest. It is our understanding that parties' ties to their social roots are to a large extent captured by these two types of linkage.

Radical left parties in Southern Europe have been selected because they constitute a well-represented and—from a linkage point of view—sufficiently representative sample of this party family in the European context. Radical left parties on the whole remain electorally relevant in Southern Europe (Table 1), which continues to be one of the main areas of European anti-capitalism (March 2011; De Waele & Seiler 2012).

In terms of pre-existing linkages, some of these parties are among the oldest and most established in their respective party systems (AKEL, KKE, PCP) with deep social roots and entrenched practices of democratic centralism. Others have emerged more recently as a consequence of the change that several communist parties have

Table 1 National Election Results of Radical Left Parties in Southern Europe (1989–2012, %)

	Cyprus	Greece		Italy		Portugal		Spain
	AKEL	KKE	SYN	PRC	PdCI	PCP	BE	IU
1989		13.1						9.1
1989		11.0						
1990		10.3						
1991	30.6					8.8		
1992				5.6				
1993		4.5	2.9					9.5
1994				6.1				
1995						8.6		
1996	33.0	5.6	5.1	8.6				10.5
1999						9.0	2.4	
2000		5.5	3.2					5.4
2001	34.7			5.0	1.7			
2002						6.9	2.7	
2004		5.9	3.3					4.9
2005						7.5	6.3	
2006	31.1			5.8	2.3			
2007		8.2	5.0					
2008				3.1				3.8
2009		7.5	4.6			7.9	9.8	
2011	32.7					7.9	5.2	6.9
2012		8.5	16.8					
2012		4.5	26.7					
Average	32.4	7.7	8.5	5.7	2.0	8.1	5.3	7.2
Total radical left	32.4	13.8		6.4		11.9		7.2

Sources: Cyprus: www.parties-and-elections.de; Greece: Greek Ministry of the Interior; Italy: www.parties-and-elections.de; Portugal: Comissão Nacional de Eleições (National Electoral Commission); Spain: Spanish Ministry of Interior and www.historiaelectoral.com.
Notes: The average for the total left in Greece does not include the vote obtained by Δημοκρατική Αριστερά (Democratic Left, DL) in the 2012 election. For the 2008 Italian election we consider the vote for the coalition Sinistra Arcobaleno (Rainbow Left, SA). The FDS and SEL will compete for the first time in the 2013 Italian national election.

experienced over the last two decades. This is the case of 'renewer' communist parties in Italy, Spain and Greece (PRC, IU, SYN) which implemented significant ideological and organisational transformations after (or just before) the fall of the Berlin Wall.[2] Finally, BE and SEL constitute very recent formations with scant organisational roots and strong reliance on 'new politics' issues and the new social media for their interaction with civil society.

The timeframe adopted spans two decades and is delimited by two major events: the fall of the Berlin Wall and the advent of the 2008–12 global economic crisis. Linkage strategies are arduous enterprises whose study requires that we take a long-term view in order to trace their evolution. As seen in the chapters in this special issue, the linkage strategies that parties pursue are usually explicitly launched at a certain point in time—most often in the context of a party conference—as public statements of parties' willingness to reconnect to their grassroots. These statements go hand in hand with the introduction of organisational reforms that parties undertake in order to be able to pursue linkage more effectively. Two decades are a sufficient period of time over which the development of such strategies can be observed.

As to the events that frame the specific time period selected, the fall of the Berlin Wall was a crucial turning point for the parties of the radical left, which—along with their strategy, programmatic offer and organisation—is likely to have rendered them prone to reconsidering their links to grassroots (March 2011). The current economic crisis seems to be marking another crucial turning point in the radical left parties' approach to linkage, given the extent of social mobilisation that the harsh austerity policies have generated. Nowhere are these latest developments more pronounced than in Southern Europe. However, making sense of radical left parties' attempts to enhance linkage to individuals and groups over the last few years, when the economic crisis hit the region, will only be possible against the background of the linkage strategies that radical left parties have developed over the past two decades.

The Importance of Social Roots: Why Radical Left Parties Launch Linkage Strategies

The country case studies in this special issue demonstrate that all South European radical left parties have initiated linkage strategies over the period studied (Table 2). Linkage strategies have been launched in the context of a founding party congress (PRC in 1991, PdCI in 1998, BE in 1999, FDS and SEL in 2008, SYRIZA in 2012), a re-founding congress (AKEL 1993, IU 2010) or a congress that embeds a party in the context of a stable political coalition with other usually much smaller parties, groups, movements and individuals of the radical left (IU in 1987, SYRIZA in 2001). In other cases linkage strategies have been initiated in the context of a party joining a broader social platform such as the Social Forum (PCP in 2003) or founding a new ancillary organisation (KKE in 1999). At this point, the objection might be made that it is very difficult to establish exactly when a party decides to initiate a new attempt to pursue linkage. It is indeed very likely that the decision has been taken in advance and is only

Table 2 Linkage Strategies Launched by South European Radical Left Parties (1987–2012)

	Leninist parties				'Renewer' parties				New parties	
	AKEL	KKE	PCP	PdCI	SYN/SYRIZA	PRC	FDS	IU	BE	SEL
1987			x					x		
1989										
1991						x				
1993	x									
1998				x						
1999		x	x			x		x	x	
2001					x					
2003			x							
2008							x			x
2010								x		
2011			x						x	
2012		x			x		x			

publicly announced in a congress or expressed in a particular party initiative. Nonetheless, we will take these key events as relatively reliable approximations. They are significant political events that radical left parties deliberately use in order to signal that they have decided to 'return to grassroots'.

With regard to the question of why radical left parties in Southern Europe launch linkage strategies, four patterns become apparent from the comparative analysis of the case studies in this special issue. These patterns point to specific factors that are likely to be decisive.

The first pattern that emerges from our case studies is that *all* the radical left parties examined have enhanced their efforts to reach out to their social roots over the past two decades. This implies that linkage is important to the party family as a whole by virtue of its ideology. In historical terms, communist parties pursued the tight encapsulation of members and the development of strong and wide organisational ties to specific segments of civil society in order to form 'counter-societies' (Kriegel 1972). The pursuit of strong links to their grassroots was closely related to their need to rely on extra-institutional mobilisation, given their exclusion from and their suspicion of the state apparatus. It was equally related to their ideology and organisational philosophy, according to which the very aim of the party was to unite and direct the class struggle of the proletariat (Lenin [1902] 1963). All radical left parties have inherited this legacy which emphasises the importance of social roots not only in their discourse but also as a central element of their internal functioning.

This ideological appeal has been an important asset for radical left parties in order to mobilise and encapsulate specific groups through their organisations. In other words, despite their increasingly office-seeking orientation, radical left parties remain parties for which ideological consistency is of paramount importance (Charalambous, in press) and whose appeal continues to make reference to championing the interests and values of a particular social constituency (Allern 2010, p. 295). As Lipset and

Rokkan have shown (1967, pp. 1–64), strengthening the ideological and organisational bonds between radical left parties and 'their' social constituency enhances party legitimacy by reinforcing partisan alignments and members' identification. Pursuing linkage to citizens and organised groups that share the party's goals, values and ideas is thus a stable, long-term priority for radical left parties as a party family insofar as ideological consistency and constituency representation remain central to their legitimacy. Despite the claim made by scholars that by the late 1980s radical left parties had distanced themselves from civil society (Lazar 1988), the articles in this special issue demonstrate that they continue to attempt to maintain proximity to their social roots and to build their appeal on specific 'natural collectivities'.

The second pattern that can be discerned can be associated with the fact that a certain class of external events seems to play some part in 'triggering' radical left parties' prioritisation of linkage. Most of the instances we have identified when radical left parties have initiated linkage strategies took place in the late 1990s after the rise of the 'global justice movement' (GJM) (SYN, KKE, BE, PCP, PRC) and/or very recently, after the sovereign debt crisis in 2010–11 (SYRIZA, KKE, IU, BE, PCP). The rise of the GJM was the first international event that brought the left's agenda to the fore in a decade, with at least some radical left parties attempting to update and reconsider that agenda from a global point of view (Della Porta 2007). The economic crisis has brought the critique of the policies of austerity to the fore and is forcing the radical left to put forth its own anti-neoliberal agenda. In both cases, the high levels of social protest that ensued rendered the pursuit of linkage to the mobilised sectors a challenge and an opportunity for the South European radical left. This should not come as a surprise to party scholars: parties may be conservative organisations but they are able to adapt to transformations in their external environment by introducing organisational change (Harmel & Janda 1994; Panebianco 1988). Such change may include innovation in the way parties organise linkage to their social roots. Clearly, the events that affect radical left parties' linkage strategy are the ones that resonate with key features of their ideology. Their continued emphasis on policy-seeking and ideology means that radical left parties' legitimacy is affected by external events that question, confirm or highlight their core principles and agenda. When radical left parties' legitimacy is in question as a result of such events, they seem to re-emphasise their links to their grassroots.

A third significant pattern can be associated with parties' responses to electoral incentives in the national political arena. Some cases in our sample can be explained in terms of party responses to electoral downturns. In particular, in the case of the PCP and IU in the late 1980s, as well as SYN and the KKE in the late 1990s, the parties of the radical left reacted to poor electoral performance by introducing new forms of linkage and relying on new forms of extra-parliamentary mobilisation. Parties' capacity to control their environment and stabilise influence over their 'social turf' continues to be a key to their survival (Panebianco 1988). Even if in the short term radical left parties do not necessarily expect a renewed emphasis on linkage to result in an immediate trade-off in votes (Allern 2010), they can be expected to signal their prioritisation of linkage after a particularly significant loss of votes. This may be thought of not so much as a knee-jerk reaction and more as a first step in a long-term strategy whereby deepening bonds with the party grassroots will help translate symbolic change into electoral gains.

A fourth and final pattern that can shed light on the question of why radical left parties launch linkage strategies is discernible in their responses to changes in national party competition. In Portugal, the PCP attempted to differentiate its ties to civil society, particularly in terms of revisiting its environmental linkage strategy, in order to prevent the further electoral advance of BE at its own expense at the turn of the twenty-first century. In much the same way, the Cypriot AKEL had modified its participatory linkages in the early 1990s in order to prevent membership defection and the electoral rise of a 'renewer' competitor, the Ανανεωτικό Δημοκρατικό Σοσιαλιστικό Κίνημα (Renewalist Democratic Socialist Movement, ADISOK). Moreover, newer radical left parties with weak social roots can be expected to be more vulnerable to the lack of organisational resources than established ones (Kitschelt 2006). The struggle for the mobilisation of new sectors and the attempt to appeal to groups with previous loyalties will lead newer parties to adopt a more aggressive, competitive strategy. This was the case with the emergence of the BE in 1999, as well as with SEL and FDS in 2008. In contrast to new parties, established radical left parties with traditional ties to a particular constituency and particular groups may take those links for granted, neglecting the pursuit of linkage.

The tendency to strengthen linkage when adopting or returning to an oppositional role is also related to the radical left parties' competitive strategy. In some of the cases studied in this volume, it seems that when radical left parties pursue office they tend to de-emphasise linkage, or at least not stress it to the same extent as when they follow an oppositional strategy. This pattern is discernible in the trajectories of both parties of the Greek left: SYN and the KKE neglected linkage over most of the 1990s, when they prioritised office-seeking, but they re-emphasised linkage when their strategy became oppositional and protest oriented. In a similar vein, the PRC prioritised linkage with social movements while taking an oppositional role, but was less able to pursue these links consistently when the party decided to participate in the centre-left coalition government headed by Romano Prodi in 2006. This pattern is also detectable in party attitudes towards linkage over the current economic crisis. The case studies in this special issue reveal a distinction between AKEL (a party in charge of a government forced to implement severe austerity measures) and SEL (which seeks participation in a future centre-left coalition), on the one hand, and the radical left parties that are in opposition, on the other one. While the latter have all reinvigorated their linkage strategies and actively tried to link to the new actors that have arisen out of Southern Europe's new politics of protest, the former have found themselves in fairly awkward positions with regard to linkage (see the section on the financial crisis below).

To summarise, all radical left parties in Southern Europe have engaged at least once in launching linkage strategies over the last two decades. In some cases this can be attributed to responses to external events, electoral incentives or changes in the dynamics of party competition. In all cases, as we argued, it is first and foremost their ideological legacy which dictates their constant concern with linkage. It is part and parcel of their ideology that they must be seen to represent the interests, ideas and values of a particular constituency. Failing to do so would damage their legitimacy.

Participatory and Environmental Linkages of the South European Radical Left

As shown in the previous section, all of the parties studied in the chapters of this volume have launched explicit linkage strategies over the past two decades. In all cases—with the exception of the PCP—this has been marked by the introduction of organisational innovations that would enable them to pursue participatory and/or environmental linkage more effectively (Table 3). This section demonstrates that there are persistent differences among radical left parties in Southern Europe with regard to the way they pursue linkage, mirrored in distinct types of organisational innovation. Divergence, it will be argued, can be explained in terms of party legacy and organisational trajectory (Allern 2010; Verge 2012).

With regard to participatory linkage, AKEL, the KKE and the PCP continue to operate on the principle that the party leadership should remain all powerful vis-à-vis party members, while implementing—to varying degrees—internal change aimed at retaining the encapsulation of members and building or maintaining a compact and self-contained subculture. Similarly, the PdCI, founded in 1998 as a minority 'orthodox' split from the 'movementist' PRC, reproduced the traditional mass party structure based on democratic centralism (Bordandini & Di Virgilio 2007). Since the late 1990s, the KKE has undergone a profound 're-bolshevisation' in terms of its reinstatement of the organisational principles of democratic centralism (Tsakatika & Eleftheriou, this volume). AKEL experienced a limited internal reorganisation in the early 1990s which allowed its members greater participation rights, while maintaining a veto for key decisions at the higher echelons of the party. The aim was to strengthen the new leadership both within and outside the party, increasing its legitimacy through the implementation of more democratic rules (Charalambous & Christophorou, this volume). The PCP, on the other hand, has not introduced any significant changes in the way it exercises participatory linkage over the democratic period and has thus continued to abide by the principles of democratic centralism, despite an alarming number of dissidents leaving the party (Jalali & Lisi 2012).

IU, BE, SYN/SYRIZA and PRC (as well as FDS and SEL) have implemented significant innovations in the way they organise the participation of their members and in the decision-making rights they allocate to members and supporters. Their aim has been to stimulate bottom-up participation of members and achieve greater involvement of supporters. This was particularly evident in the case of PRC, which broke with the mass party tradition based on the active role of party members and favoured the participation of sympathisers and less committed militants. The new organisational structure not only accepted internal dissent and distinct political

Table 3 Innovations Associated with Linkage Strategies (1987–2012)

	Participatory linkage	Environmental linkage
AKEL	Increased members' rights in candidate selection	Introducing recognisable candidates from civil society organisations
KKE	'Re-bolshevisation', re-structuring cells on a sectoral basis	Establishment of new ancillary trade union, 'popular committees'
PCP	No significant changes	Pursuit of links to social forum (SF)
PdCI	No significant changes	Establishing links to trade unions and SF
SYN/SYRIZA	Members' referendum for selecting MEP (member of the European Parliament) candidates	Left coalition, SF, SYN Youth engagement with new social movements, support for solidarity initiatives
PRC	Party 'circles' and drawing of manifestos with participation of both members and sympathisers	Establishing links to social movements (SM), SF, emphasis on extra-parliamentary mobilisation, links to trade unions
FDS	'Houses of the left', 'confederal' structure	No significant changes
IU	Members' participation in drawing up manifestos (*areas*), primaries	Left coalition, SF, social platforms
BE	No formal leadership, rotation in office	SF, active support of SM in the parliamentary arena; high levels of membership/leadership overlap with SM
SEL	'Nichi's factories'	New types of mobilisation ('mail bombing', 'flash mobs')

traditions, but also aimed to build a network with social groups through forms of participatory democracy—for instance, in the elaboration of party manifestos (De Nardis 2005). This development can also be seen in IU's statutory provision for candidate selection primaries and its thematic *áreas* aimed at opening up party policy-making to all members, non-members and social movements (described by Ramiro and Verge, this volume), both foundational principles of IU from the late 1980s.

Likewise, SYN members' referenda to establish the order of candidates for the European Parliament (EP) on the party lists, an innovation introduced in 1992 (Tsakatika 2010), and the BE's application since 1999 of principles of 'polyarchic' leadership, MPs' rotation and intra-party democracy serve the same purpose. The openness of both FDS and SEL in terms of policy-making input, i.e. through the local 'Houses of the Left',[5] thematic fora and referenda as well as the SEL leader's online support circles (Fabbriche di Nichi), is a more recent expression of the same imperative of empowering party members. In practice, SEL seems to be more effective in implementing the new forms of participatory linkage than FDS, although the impetus towards greater openness has diminished during the Monti government (see below). New modes of mobilisation have also been adopted as part of broadening individual members' repertoire of participation beyond traditional party structures, involving practices such as 'mail-bombing' and 'flash mobs' (Bordandini, this volume). Furthermore, some of these parties have been actively encouraging the politicisation of their younger cohorts through novel channels, for instance by supporting their involvement in new social movements and solidarity initiatives, as shown by SYN Youth in Greece and the BE in Portugal. For all six parties, empowering members in party decision-making has been a genuine aim but in practice it has often encountered obstacles due to the overwhelming strength of factions (SYN, IU, BE, PRC, FDS) or the leadership (BE, SEL).

Moving on to environmental linkage, AKEL, the PCP, the KKE and the PdCI have aimed to guide civil society organisations from the top down through their ancillary organisations, to which they lay exclusive claim; they follow the traditional 'transmission belt' model associated with parties based on the Leninist model, which sees the party as a political and intellectual vanguard meant to educate the masses (Table 4). Their primary focus is on trade unions, where the party by and large directs the political aims and the mobilisation strategy of its ancillary organisations. AKEL, the KKE and the PCP are all highly successful in maintaining formal or quasi-formal, stable and enduring ties to the Παγκύπρια Εργατική Ομοσπονδία (Pan-Cyprian Labour Federation, PEO), the Πανεργατικό Αγωνιστικό Μέτωπο (All Workers Militant Front, PAME) and the Confederação Geral dos Trabalhadores Portugueses (General Confederation of Portuguese Workers, CGTP), respectively. The PdCI had also sought to establish strong organisational ties to the largest Italian trade union, the Confederazione Generale Italiana del Lavoro (Italian General Confederation of Labour, CGIL), with limited success.

AKEL is singular in this respect among current European radical left parties, as it not only dominates the trade union movement but also maintains an extraordinary

Table 4 Participatory and Environmental Linkage

	Participatory linkage			Environmental linkage		
	Direction	Strength	Range	Direction	Strength	Range
Leninist parties						
AKEL	Top-down/DC	High	Members	Top-down	High	Broad and exclusive
KKE	Top-down/DC	High	Members	Top-down	High	Exclusive, TUs
PCP	Top-down/DC	High	Members	Top-down	High	Exclusive, TUs
PdCI	Top-down/DC	High	Members	Top-down	High	Exclusive, TUs
'Renewer' parties						
SYN/SYRIZA	Bottom-up	Moderate	Members	Mutual	Moderate/informal	Broad, SMs + TUs
PRC	Bottom-up	Moderate	Members/supporters	Mutual	Moderate/informal	Broad, SMs
FDS	Bottom-up	Moderate	Members/supporters	Mutual	Moderate/informal	Broad, SMs + TUs
IU	Bottom-up	Moderate	Members/supporters	Mutual	Moderate/informal	Broad, SMs + TUs
New parties						
BE	Bottom-up	Moderate/loose	Members/supporters	Mutual	Moderate– weak/informal	Privileged, SMs
SEL	Bottom-up/e-democracy	Loose	Members/supporters	Mutual	Moderate– weak/informal	Broad and non-exclusive

Note: DC = democratic centralism; TU = trade union; SM = social movement.

network of other ancillary organisations within civil society organisations that reach every nook and cranny of Cypriot society, including youth and women's associations, cultural and athletic activities, farmers' organisations and the business sector. It has also reached out to sectors of civil society, such as environmental NGOs, which are to be found outside the range of its own ancillary structures. Over the last decade the KKE has restructured its entire party organisation in order to accommodate the needs of its ancillary trade union, PAME, while remaining extremely critical of social movements, such as the GJM, over which it has no influence. As shown by Lisi (this volume), the PCP has also prioritised its links to the main trade union. It did take small and reluctant steps towards approaching the new social movements in the early 2000s, but only when it became clear that its failure to engage with them would benefit its main competitor. The election in 2012 of a former member of the PCP's Central Committee as the new secretary-general of the CGTP confirmed the continued influence of the party over the trade union movement. All three parties generally favour more traditional modes of mobilisation, such as strikes and mass demonstrations, and tend to distrust or to rely little on social movements or activist practices.

The pioneering experience of the PRC was of the utmost importance for the evolution of environmental linkage between South European radical left parties and the new social movements. In this respect, the PRC model influenced all the parties examined in this special issue, with the exception of the KKE, the PCP and AKEL. In accordance with the organisational transformation and ideological renewal implemented after the IV Congress (1999), the PRC aimed to break with the democratic centralist tradition, establishing organic, strong, less exclusive and more mutual ties to social movements and independent trade unions (*comitati di base*), 'internalising' the movement experience and reinvigorating its political action and mobilisation practices (De Nardis 2005; Bordandini & Di Virgilio 2007).

Drawing on the PRC model, environmental linkage between SYN, IU, BE, FDS, SEL and the new social movements has since mostly taken place informally through loose leadership and membership overlap and in the case of SYN/SYRIZA through the establishment of a connective role for social solidarity initiatives or by providing a bridge that links the movements together. These ties are also used to further parties' aims of recruiting cadres and integrating members: they may be seen as a 'functional equivalent' or substitute for the mass party subculture. Radical left parties' links to social movements may be mostly informal but, contrary to what some scholars assume (Poguntke 2002), they are not necessarily weak. They are often enduring despite variation in levels of social movement mobilisation over time. BE, SYN, IU, FDS and SEL (as well as the PRC before them) adopt, articulate and champion the 'new politics' claims of these movements in the political arena. They gain in terms of legitimacy by presenting themselves to the electorate as the social movements' privileged and reliable allies.

More formal interactions between these parties and the social movements have also been advanced through the coalition strategy (IU, SYRIZA) and participation in social platforms alongside other organisations of civil society such as (but not exclusively) the national social fora (BE, SYN, IU and PRC in the past). This change was related to a shift in mobilisation strategy, aiming to broaden participation to non-members ('independents') and to institutionalise cooptation of friendly civic organisations.

With the exception of SEL, which according to its delegates does not look for close or exclusive ties to particular trade unions (despite promoting the unity of the trade union movement in Italy), all the parties examined pursue preferential links with trade unions, alongside their commitment to develop and maintain links to new social movements. While SYN has gone down the route of setting up its own rudimentary collateral organisation in the labour movement and the FDS has built privileged links to the CGIL, the IU and BE have preferred to rely more on membership and cadre overlap in the unions closest to them, the now fully independent Comissiones Obreras (Workers' Commissions, CCOO) in Spain and the PCP-dominated CGTP in Portugal, respectively. However, newer parties such as BE have experienced considerable difficulty in developing links to established labour organisations. BE, SYN and SEL (as well as the PRC before them) are open to direct collaboration with base-level labour committees that are not necessarily part of the official trade union confederations.

With regard to the direction (Duverger [1951] 1964), strength and exclusivity of linkage (Allern 2010), our findings show that there is considerable variation in the way party linkages are pursued within the radical left party family (Table 4). On the one hand, parties adhering to the Leninist tradition—such as AKEL, the KKE, the PCP and the PdCI—have established top-down linkages with their members and civil society organisations, with strong and exclusive ties. On the other hand, 'renewer' and newer parties have preferred mutual, looser and less exclusive links with organised groups. They have promoted 'new politics' issues and the bottom-up participation of their members and supporters. Although they have attempted to build strong ties with civil society and have often introduced marked organisational innovations, in practice the informal character of this relationship has led to weaker and less stable links than those developed by democratic centralist parties. Overall, these results confirm the importance of the organisational trajectory on the type of linkages pursued by radical left parties.

Linkage in the Financial Crisis: The Radical Left Divided?

The adverse social effects of the recent economic crisis have triggered high levels of civil society mobilisation against the South European governing parties, constrained to apply painful austerity measures and structural reforms. The factors that were identified in the previous sections as explaining why (ideology, external events, electoral incentives and party competition) and how (history and organisational trajectory) radical left parties pursue participatory and environmental linkage go a long way towards explaining their responses over the crisis period.

AKEL is the only radical left party in Europe that is currently in charge of government under crisis conditions. It finds itself constrained to implement austerity measures and extensive structural reforms under pressure from markets, credit rating agencies and EU fiscal norms as much as other governments in the region. AKEL seems to be using its linkages to civil society organisations to pacify the wave of social protest that could potentially arise, as noted by Charalambous and Christophorou (this volume).

The Italian case highlights the fact that, in addition to government incumbency, an office-seeking strategy may also limit the mobilisation potential of the radical left. While FDS has displayed a strong opposition to the Monti government, contesting not only the austerity measures but also labour and pension reforms, liberalisation policies and the dismantlement of the public sector, SEL has adopted a more moderate position given a prospective alliance with the main centre-left party, Partito Democratico (Democratic Party, PD). Despite its (inevitable) reliance on extra-parliamentary mobilisation, SEL has agreed to sign an agreement with the PD for the next general elections (scheduled for spring 2013). This has caused some disgruntlement within the party, which demonstrates the difficulties involved in combining office- and policy-seeking objectives.

Radical left parties in Greece, Spain and Portugal have put up strong opposition to government measures and have taken to the streets alongside trade unions and social movements. IU is supportive of strike action organised by the main trade unions, but seems to be having trouble connecting to the social movements that have emerged in response to the crisis. Despite the fact that there was a higher proportion of IU members among participants in the Indignados (Indignants) movement[3] than of members of other parties (Martín 2012), the anti-party character of the movement and the wait-and-see strategy adopted by the IU leadership have been obstacles to the IU assuming a leading role in the mobilisation of civil society, even in times of crisis.[4]

The BE and SYN/SYRIZA are involved in social mobilisation, supporting the new social movements, activist practices and solidarity initiatives such as the Indignados that have arisen in response to cuts and labour reforms, articulating their claims in the political sphere and pursuing a mutual partnership with them. On the other hand, the PCP and the KKE have put all their weight behind trade union protests and strikes and tried to steer popular mobilisation through their ancillary organisations. They have not connected to the new social movements, the KKE going as far as to reject them as little more than a distraction from the main aims of the class struggle. While in Portugal radical left parties are finding it difficult to connect to new social movements because, much like in Spain, they are confronting generalised attitudes of scepticism and anti-partyism, the Greek radical left is facing a completely different situation. The June 2012 elections brought about an overhaul of the Greek political system and system of interest representation, SYRIZA being the main beneficiary in terms of votes, and individual supporters and trade unionists (from the broader centre-left) joining its ranks en masse. Tsakatika and Eleftheriou (this volume) argue that SYRIZA's internal pluralism and unitary approach to environmental linkage have strengthened its legitimacy and credibility and given it a clear advantage over its longstanding competitor, the KKE.

Conclusions

The studies of South European radical left parties' linkages which populate this special issue have not confirmed the claim that parties are turning their backs on their members and organised groups. On the contrary, findings add to the comparative literature that stresses the importance parties attribute to prioritising these links. From a comparative perspective, ideology emerges as a key factor in explaining the extent to which parties prioritise linkage. Despite profound differences within the party family, all radical left parties pursue linkage because this is part of their ideological core and very raison d'être. Moreover, they have pursued linkage in ways that have resonated with their legacy, introducing changes with the aim of maintaining or reinforcing their political identities, as well as their normative conception of democracy. This finding indicates that Lipset and Rokkan's (1967) cleavage-based approach may well continue to be a relevant lens with which to assess linkage, and the comparative study of linkage across party families a fruitful pursuit if we wish to make sense of variation. Further research could explore, for instance, the possibility that party families such as the Greens and the extreme right whose ideology also emphasises ties to the grassroots are as inclined to pursue linkage as the radical left party family.

Our findings only partially confirm the general trends in the evolution of European parties' participatory and environmental linkages, involving, respectively, the trend towards internal party democratisation and the trend towards the establishment of looser and broader links between political parties and organisations of civil society. While democratic centralist parties in Southern Europe (PCP, KKE, AKEL) deviate from the trend of allocating greater decision-making rights to members, 'renewer' and newer parties converge, as they have a strong commitment to grassroots' participation and intra-party democracy. In terms of environmental linkage, the Leninist parties remain vanguardist and thus deviate from the general trend that sees the rise of more informal and less exclusive links. Developments in SEL, FDS, BE, SYN/SYRIZA and IU demonstrate that these parties do attempt to relate on a more mutual basis to a multitude of groups and introduce important organisational innovations that reinforce the role of parties as 'receivers' rather than 'transmitters' (Katz & Mair 2012). However, 'renewer' and newer parties of the South European radical left still generally prefer to maintain strong (though informal) ties to a limited number of groups, namely those they see as more representative of, or whose interests they interpret as being akin to, those of their social constituencies. They aim to be seen as the privileged political 'representatives' of social movements and trade unions rather than simply one of the latter's political contacts. Further comparative research is required to explore whether these findings can be generalised to radical left parties in other countries in Europe and beyond.

Acknowledgements

The authors would like to thank Luke March, Donatella Della Porta, André Freire, Manos Matsaganis and the editors of South European Society and Politics for valuable comments on previous drafts.

Myrto Tsakatika would like to acknowledge financial support from the Caledonian Research Foundation which assisted in the completion of this project.

Notes

[1] SYRIZA is a political coalition between SYN and a number of small groups, social movements and parties of the Greek extra-parliamentary left which was forged in 2001, remained an electoral coalition between 2004 and 2012 and was transformed into a unified party on the eve of the June 2012 legislative elections.

[2] With the term 'renewer' communist parties we emphasise the organisational changes that these parties have undertaken since the collapse of communism. Therefore, our classification does not follow the distinction between 'conservative' and 'reform' communist parties elaborated by March (2011, pp. 16–19), which is based mainly on the ideological evolution of this party family.

[3] The Indignados movement, initiated by Spanish protestors in Madrid on 14 May 2011, rapidly spread to Greece and other European countries. It demanded the reversal of austerity policies, and direct democracy. Their protest has involved mass demonstrations and open assemblies in central squares of large urban centres.

[4] We would like to thank Luis Ramiro and Tània Verge on this point.

[5] The 'Houses of the Left' were local structures with the aim to gather contributions from civil society and coordinate and mobilise different types of associations and organisations, as well as underprivileged social groups (immigrants, young, evicted, etc.). They emerged with the birth of the Rainbow Left and then recognised in the FDS' statutes as a central component of its organisation.

References

Aarts, K. (1995) 'Intermediate organizations and interest representation', in *Citizens and the State*, eds H.-D. Klingemann & D. Fuchs, Oxford University Press, Oxford, pp. 227–257.

Allern, E. H. (2010) *Political Parties and Interest Groups in Norway*, ECPR Press, London.

Allern, E. H. & Bale, T. (2012a) 'Political parties and interest groups: disentangling complex relationships', *Party Politics*, vol. 18, no. 1, pp. 7–25.

Allern, E. H. & Bale, T. (2012b) 'Conclusion: qualifying the common wisdom', *Party Politics*, vol. 18, no. 1, pp. 99–106.

Bale, T. & Dunphy, R. (2011) 'In from the cold? Left parties and government involvement since 1989', *Comparative European Politics*, vol. 9, no. 3, pp. 269–291.

Bordandini, P. & Di Virgilio, A. (2007) 'Partito dei Comunisti Italiani. Ritratto di un partito di nicchia', *Rivista Italiana di Scienza Politica*, vol. 37, no. 2, pp. 261–296.

Bosco, A. (2000) *Comunisti. Trasformazioni di partito in Italia, Spagna e Portogallo*, Il Mulino, Bologna.

Caul Kittilson, M. & Scarrow, S. E. (2003) 'Political parties and the rhetoric and realities of democratization', in *Democracy Transformed? Expanding Political Opportunities in Advanced Industrial Democracies*, eds B. E. Cain, R. J. Dalton & S. E. Scarrow, Oxford University Press, Oxford, pp. 59–80.

Cross, W. & Blais, A. (2012) 'Who selects the party leader?', *Party Politics*, vol. 18, no. 2, pp. 127–150.

Charalambous, G. (in press) *European Integration and the Communist Dilemma. Communist Party Responses to Europe in Greece, Cyprus and Italy*, Ashgate, Farnham.

Della Porta, D. (ed.) (2007) *The Global Justice Movement: Cross-National and Transnational Perspectives*, Paradigm, Boulder, CO.

De Nardis, F. (2005) 'Sinistra in movimento. La Rifondazione Comunista dalla resistenza globale al governo di alternativa', *Quaderni di Scienza Politica*, vol. 12, no. 3, pp. 409–455.

De Waele, J. M. & Seiler, D. L. (eds) (2012) *Les partis de la gauche anticapitaliste en Europe*, Economica, Paris.

Duverger, M. ([1951] 1964) *Political Parties*, 3rd edn, Methuen, London.

Gauja, A. (2009) 'Internal party democracy and policy formulation: rationales, trends and relevance', paper presented at the European Consortium on Political Research joint sessions, 14–19 April 2009, Lisbon.

Harmel, R. & Janda, K. (1994) 'An Integrated Theory of Party Goals and Party Change', *Journal of Theoretical Politics*, vol. 1, no. 3, pp. 259–287.

Hazan, R. Y. & Rahat, G. (2010) *Democracy within Parties: Candidate Selection Methods and Their Political Consequences*, Oxford University Press, Oxford.

Katz, R. S. & Mair, P. (1995) 'Changing models of party organization and party democracy: the emergence of the cartel party', *Party Politics*, vol. 1, no. 1, pp. 5–28.

Katz, R. S. & Mair, P. (2012) 'Parties, interest groups and cartels: a comment', *Party Politics*, vol. 18, no. 1, pp. 107–111.

Kirchheimer, O. (1966) 'The transformation of the West European party systems', in *Political Parties and Political Development*, eds J. LaPalombara & M. Weiner, Princeton University Press, Princeton, NJ, pp. 177–200.

Kitschelt, H. (2006) 'Movement parties', in *Handbook of Party Politics*, eds R. Katz & W. Crotty, Sage, London, pp. 278–290.

Kriegel, A. (1972) *The French Communists: Profile of a People*, University of Chicago Press, Chicago.

Jalali, C. & Lisi, M. (2012) 'Quand le changement semble dangereux: l'évolution du Parti communiste portugais', in *Les partis de la gauche anticapitaliste en Europe*, eds J. M. De Waele & D. L. Seiler, Economica, Paris, pp. 180–204.

Lawson, K. (1980) 'Political parties and linkage', in *Political Parties and Linkage: A Comparative Perspective*, ed. K. Lawson, Yale University Press, New Haven, pp. 3–24.

Lazar, M. (1988) 'Communism in Western Europe in the 1980s', *Journal of Communist Studies*, vol. 4, no. 3, pp. 243–257.

Lenin, V. I. ([1902] 1963) *What Is to Be Done?* Oxford University Press, Oxford.

Lipset, S. M. & Rokkan, S. (eds) (1967) *Party Systems and Voter Alignments*, Free Press, New York.

March, L. (2011) *Radical Left Parties in Contemporary Europe*, Routledge, London.

March, L. & Mudde, C. (2005) 'What's left of the radical left? The European radical left since 1989: decline and mutation', *Comparative European Politics*, vol. 3, no. 1, pp. 23–49.

Martín, I. (2012) 'Political disaffection revisited: the *Indignant* movement in Spain, or a different way of doing politics', paper presented at the conference 'Voting and Protesting in Europe since 2008', Georgetown University, Washington, 17–18 April

Panebianco, A. (1988) *Political Parties: Organization and Power*, Cambridge University Press, Cambridge.

Pedersen, K., Bille, L., Buch, R., Elklit, J., Hansen, B. & Nielsen, H. J. (2004) 'Sleeping or active partners? Danish party members at the turn of the millennium', *Party Politics*, vol. 10, no. 4, pp. 367–383.

Poguntke, T. (2002) 'Parties without firm social roots? Party organizational linkage', in *Political Parties in the New Europe: Political and Analytical Challenges*, eds K. Luther & F. Müller-Rommel, Oxford University Press, Oxford, pp. 43–62.

Poguntke, T. (2006) 'Political parties and other organizations', in *Handbook of Party Politics*, eds R. Katz & W. Crotty, Sage, London, pp. 396–405.

Scarrow, S. (2009) 'Political activism and party members', in *Oxford Handbook of Political Behaviour*, eds R. J. Dalton & H. P. Klingemann, Oxford University Press, Oxford, pp. 636–654.

Schwartz, M. A. (2005) 'Linkage processes in party networks', in *Political Parties and Political Systems: the Concept of Linkage Revisited*, eds A. Römmele, D. M. Farrell & P. Ignazi, Praeger, Westport, CT, pp. 37–60.

Thomas, C. (ed.) (2001) *Political Parties and Interest Groups. Shaping Democratic Governance*, Lynne Rienner, Boulder, CO.

Tsakatika, M. (2010) 'Bloco de Esquerda and Synaspismos on European Integration: organization, strategy, ideology', paper presented at the 60th PSA Conference, University of Edinburgh, 29 March.

Van Biezen, I., Mair, P. & Poguntke, T. (2011) 'Going, going ... gone? Party membership in the 21st century', *European Journal of Political Research*, vol. 51, no. 1, pp. 24–56.

Verge, T. (2012) 'Party strategies towards civil society in new democracies: the Spanish case', *Party Politics*, vol. 18, no. 1, pp. 45–60.

Warner, C. (2000) *Confessions of an Interest Group. The Catholic Church and Political Parties in Europe*, Princeton University Press, Princeton, NJ.

Yishai, Y. (2001) *Land of Paradoxes. Interest Politics in Israel*, SUNY Press, Albany.

Myrto Tsakatika (PhD Essex) is a Lecturer in Politics at the School of Social and Political Sciences, University of Glasgow. Her research interests lie in European Union and South European politics. Her latest publications appeared in international peer reviewed journals such as the Journal of Common Market Studies, *Journal of European Public Policy and Europe–Asia Studies.*

Marco Lisi is an Assistant Professor in the Department of Political Studies, Universidade Nova of Lisbon. He has published two books on Portuguese political parties and several articles on political parties and electoral behaviour in international journals such as *West European Politics, South European Society and Politics* and *Representation.*

Rediscovering Civil Society? Renewal and Continuity in the Portuguese Radical Left

Marco Lisi

The importance of party organisational models to party-civil-society relations has been substantially overlooked in the scholarly literature. Drawing on the Portuguese case, this study examines to what extent radical left parties have established different links with civil society, namely by allying with social movements and trade unions. Our findings confirm that party organisational models significantly shape the relationship between the radical left and civil society. However, external challenges and internal pressures increase the influence of party leadership in determining linkage strategies. Finally, the impact of the recent economic and financial crisis has been limited, especially in terms of programmatic and organisational renewal.

The transformations that have taken place in radical left parties since 1989 have heightened academic interest in their integration at the institutional level and the challenges of government participation (Dunphy & Bale 2011; McDonnell & Newell 2011). However, little attention has been paid to the relationship between radical left parties and civil society. This subject is crucial not only because it can shed more light on party change—especially from the organisational and programmatic point of view—but also because it can contribute to analysing party mobilisation and explaining parties' electoral successes and failures.

There is a strong relationship between party organisational models and the representation of specific demands from civil society. As Schattschneider has pointed out (1942, p. 71), '*organization is the mobilization of bias*. Some issues are organized into politics while others are organized out.' The ideological crisis and the institutional opportunities offered with the opening of the structure of competition have forced radical left parties to rethink—and, in some case, redefine—their relations with civil society and the representation of specific social groups. What are the characteristics of radical left parties' social anchorage? To what extent have party organisational models influenced the representation and mobilisation of civil society? More generally, what factors may explain party linkages to civil society?

This paper addresses these questions by considering the case of the two Portuguese radical left parties, the Partido Comunista Português (Portuguese Communist Party, PCP) and the Bloco de Esquerda (Left Bloc, BE). Traditionally, the 'anti-system' nature of both radical left parties has excluded them from government. Despite this, the electoral performance of the Portuguese radical left seems a success case in the European context, where the aggregate vote share of this party family has generally been stable since 1989 (March 2011). While the BE experienced steady electoral growth until 2009, increasing its share of the vote from 2.4 per cent in 1999 to 9.9 per cent in 2009, the PCP dramatically lost half of its support between 1983 and 1991 (from 18.1 to 8.8 per cent). It has since, over the last two decades, been able to maintain a stable electoral record. As this study will show, the linkage between radical left parties and civil society has significantly contributed to this relatively positive result by representing demands of specific social groups and mobilising new sectors.

We contend in this work that party organisational models and the strategy adopted by party leadership are important factors to explain the type of relationship between Portuguese radical left parties and civil society. We also argue that the analysis of this case is worthy of academic study because it shows that radical left parties may establish different types of party linkage to civil society, displaying different characteristics over time. This research draws on several interviews with politicians and activists from both the PCP and the BE, as well as on party documents, newspapers and surveys.

The article proceeds as follows. The next section presents the theoretical framework by discussing the relationship between radical left parties and civil society. The third section deals with party organisational models, focusing in particular on party structures and the internal distribution of power. Then the relationship between radical left parties and social movements is examined before exploring the links to trade unions in the following section. The conclusions summarise our findings and discuss the implications for radical left parties.

Models of Party Organisation and Links to Civil Society

Established parties have increasingly lost their traditional role of intermediation and the capacity to mobilise citizens through ideological platforms. The growing difficulty of representing different social groups emerges clearly if we look at two distinct arenas: the capacity to mobilise citizens through party organisations and the links established with external organisations and civic associations. The first dimension represents the 'participatory linkages', that is, the instruments parties use to foster participation and mobilisation. The second is related to 'environmental linkages', which focus on the ties with civic organisations and movements.

Several studies suggest that the organisational crisis of contemporary parties has led to a change in the type of linkages established with civil society. On the one hand, party members seem to have lost their traditional functions, as party organisations are increasingly downplaying their contribution (Katz 1990). On the other, evidence reveals that parties are out of touch with civil society due to the decline in the formal overlap between parties and civic organisations, and a tendency towards increased autonomy and loosening ties (Selle 1997; Thomas 2001; Poguntke 2002).

However, it is difficult to find a general pattern for party linkages in contemporary political parties. Firstly, there has been a trend towards more internal democracy in parties which grants individual party members increasing powers (Caul Kittilson & Scarrow 2003). Secondly, while relations between 'old' parties and social groups have generally become more distant, new and outsider parties may still be interested in establishing strong links with civil society (Allern 2010). The lack of institutional resources and the attempt to strengthen their legitimacy and to stabilise their electoral support are particularly important factors that lead to prioritising environmental linkages.

Parties present different types of incentives to foster participatory linkages, as well as distinct ties with external organisations and movements (Sartori 2005). According to previous empirical studies (Poguntke 2002; Kitschelt 2006), new parties clearly differ from more traditional party models in their types of linkages to civil society. While old parties have generally maintained their control over party members and displayed relatively stable ties with collateral organisations, new parties have attempted to cultivate closer relations between leaders and members, with more horizontal ties. Therefore, they have not only privileged internal democracy, but also informal links with social groups, giving priority to single-issue mobilisation and a strategic alliance with movements. Given these findings, we expect radical left parties characterised by mass-type organisations to be more likely to 'encapsulate' their members and to establish close and formal links with actors from civil society sharing the same ideological profile. By contrast, radical left parties with a more open organisational structure will be more prone to foster internal participation and to increase members' powers while creating more distant and broader relations with civil society.

However, the party organisational model is not the only factor influencing party–civil-society relations. The electoral environment is also relevant. The competitive arena affects the strategy adopted by radical left parties and the way they establish links with civil society (Allern & Bale 2012). The mobilisation of core voters or the strategy of electoral alliance may for example act as electoral stimuli, leading party organisations to strengthen specific ties to social groups. Moreover, the need to achieve political integration may also influence how parties relate to civic society, loosening the links with external organisations. From this point of view, party leadership plays a crucial role in interpreting the external challenges and taking strategic decisions (Thomas 2001; Poguntke 2002). Besides historical factors and organisational traditions, leaderships enjoy a certain freedom of action in all types of party. This capacity of leadership adaptation does not necessarily imply a cost–benefit calculus. It may also depend on the ideological legacy, intra-party conflicts or the internal distribution of power. Drawing on the two Portuguese radical left parties, this article aims to examine to what extent these factors influence party linkages with civil society, by analysing both their main characteristics and their evolution over the last two decades.

Party Organisations and Participatory Linkages: The Portuguese Case

Several authors have pointed out that the core features of party organisations are extremely important not only because the organisational structure is a crucial element that allows parties to establish links to organised associations and represent social groups, but also because it helps examine the instruments and the type of mobilisation (Panebianco 1988; Katz & Mair 1995). Below, we will show how the two radical left parties differ with regard to organisational models and intra-party functioning. This will allow us to examine the characteristics of participatory linkages and their evolution over time.

The PCP was the only party founded before the fall of the dictatorship and one of the main actors of the revolution period. The crucial role it played in those years strengthened the solid and extensive organisation built during the authoritarian regime, increasing its level of institutionalisation. Therefore, given the catch-all character of the main governing parties, the PCP can be regarded as the only mass party in the Portuguese political system (Jalali 2007). Its organisational model is based on the traditional structure of communist parties, characterised by 'democratic centralism'. Although this method is supposed to transmit the preferences of the lower echelons to the national party bodies, in practice the organisational structure functions according to top-down hierarchical ties. Party leadership and party officials control the election of the main national party bodies (the central committee, the secretariat and the political commission), the formation of factions is prohibited and congress decisions are binding.

This model has remained fairly stable over the democratic period, with 'democratic centralism' as the main overarching principle of party functioning. In particular, party leadership has traditionally controlled both the elaboration of the party programme and the recruitment process. First, congresses are usually allowed to vote only on a single programme and a single list for the central committee, both controlled by the party leadership. Second, the main party bodies (secretariat and political commission) exert a tight control over elected officials, as well as over party structures at lower levels (Cunha 1992).

As for the relationship with civil society, the PCP has followed the traditional communist model and established an organic linkage with ancillary organisations. In addition to the historical links with trade unions (see below), the PCP has maintained privileged relations with the *Confederação Nacional de Agricultores* (Agriculture National Confederation, CNA), the National Confederation of Pensioners and Elders (MURPI) and several cooperative associations. Otherwise, the most important ancillary organisations are the youth and women organisations (*Juventude Comunista Portuguesa and Movimento Democrático de Mulheres*, respectively), and the *União de Estudantes Comunistas* (Communist Student Union, UEC).

The BE's organisational model presents completely distinct features. The BE originated from two small left-extremist parties (Partido Socialista Revolucionário [PSR] and União Democrática Popular [UDP]) and a group of communist dissidents (Política XXI).[1] The new party resembled the left-libertarian parties outlined by Kitschelt (1988). The influence of social movements on its genetic model was clear from the outset. The founding parties that gave rise to this new political actor aimed to create something different from 'traditional' (left) parties. In its founding constitution, the BE was defined as a 'political movement of citizens' based on a civic culture of participation with the goal of finding alternatives to capitalism (BE 2000). Social movements were a great inspiration in defining the main features of this new political force.[2]

The strong influence of social movements is also clear when we examine the organisational structure and the decision-making process. Like other movement parties (Kitschelt 2006), the BE decided to implement a configuration centred on horizontal links between members and higher echelons and on participatory and decentralised mechanisms of decision-making. Contrary to the rigid vertical model that characterises the PCP, the BE adopted a loose membership and a low level of structural articulation based on a network organisation. Moreover, the lack of a clear leadership with the adoption of a 'poliarchic' executive was another important distinction between the two parties. The purpose of this choice was to maintain a substantial degree of autonomy for the several founding parties, while representing the pluralism of the new political force.

After the success obtained in the 2005 legislative election, a new party statute introduced two important changes (Lisi 2009). The first was a reorganisation of national party bodies. Besides the creation of an executive organ (political committee), the figure of a coordinator emerged through the leadership of Francisco Louçã, a former member of the PSR, who is the de facto leader and the figure with the greatest visibility and popularity among the public and the media. However, it is worth noting that party statutes still do not formally recognise this role or determine the competences of the secretariat, which is the body responsible for executive coordination of everyday activities.

The second main change focused on party structure, with the creation of vertical links between the national and local party level. These organisational changes had two main effects. On the one hand, there was an increase in the level of centralisation. On the other, this reform aimed to strengthen party institutionalisation, especially in terms of internal cohesion and unity. The result is that internal incentives to participate have weakened, while party leadership has enhanced its control over both party members and the party in public office.[3]

These different models of party organisations had two important effects. The first involves the encapsulation of party members. While the PCP has been characterised by a strong grassroots structure, active mobilisation and the integration of its members into party organs, the BE has displayed weak societal roots and increasing difficulty in converting its electoral growth into a stable party base. Although the BE's social base has substantially grown over the last decade, membership figures are significantly lower than those of the PCP (Lisi 2011). Moreover, if we observe the ratio between members and voters, it is easy to see that while the BE's electoral base is quite flexible and varies significantly according to the party's electoral performance, the PCP still displays the highest membership density despite the remarkable loss of members over the last decade (from 131,000 members in 2001 to 59,000 in 2009). This factor may also partially explain the poor electoral record of the BE in the 2011 legislative elections (5.2 per cent).

The horizontal relationship between party elites is another important difference between the two models of party organisation. The PCP has tried to maintain a united image bordering on unanimity, especially when several internal conflicts emerged with the fall of communism (Bosco 2001). Strong criticisms came to light with regard to party organisation and strategy, with several leaders defending the need for party reform. However, the reformists have been unable to present a unitary position or gain enough support within the party. This inevitably led to the failure of the attempts to reform the party from within, prompting the exit of reformers after the XVI and XVII congresses (2002 and 2004, respectively).

In contrast to the cohesion of the PCP's dominant coalition, factionalism has become an important part of how the BE functions. The founding parties of the BE have maintained their control over the internal distribution of power, thus marginalising the influence of independents within the party.[4] In practice, the three main components represent clear identifiable factions, as shown by the fact that whereas Louçã has always occupied the leadership position the leadership of the parliamentary group has usually been allocated to one of the other founding groups (UDP or Política XXI). Moreover, the representation within the main party bodies privileges the four main factions to the detriment of more recent party members who joined the party directly and without any previous affiliation. The prevalence of organised factions within the party was an important factor that demobilised members and limited both leadership and programmatic renovation.[5]

The overall picture of the organisational model adopted by Portuguese radical left parties reveals two distinct genetic models. While social movements and left-libertarian parties clearly influenced the BE's organisational identity, the PCP has preserved the traditional communist organisation. The former has strongly emphasised participatory linkages, whereas the latter has offered members little incentive to influence intra-party decisions. The organisational development, however, has led the BE to function more in line with traditional hierarchical mechanisms, limiting the participatory linkages. The next sections complement this analysis by considering environmental linkages, that is, the relationship with both social movements and trade unions.

The Relationship between Radical Left Parties and Social Movements

After the end of the dictatorship, the emergence and activation of varied social movements brought a wide range of new demands to light. During that period, the radical left remained extremely fragmented and supported the (often spontaneous) mobilisation that took place from the bottom up, which contrasted strongly with the more hierarchical and institutional orientation adopted by the PCP. Despite the widespread popular movements, the consolidation of the new political system led to the demobilisation of civil society, as shown by the low levels of associational membership (Viegas, Faria & Santos 2010).

Two characteristics have marked the relationship between radical left parties and civil society in the democratic period: the weakness of social movements and civic organisations and their dependency on political parties and institutional resources (Santos 1994; Cruz 1995). On the one hand, the lack of strong leadership, the low levels of civic engagement, and low visibility in the media have made the emergence of social movements very difficult. As a consequence, established political parties have traditionally acted as mobilising actors, especially when left parties have been able to coopt leaders' organisations and incorporate their main demands into policy platforms. On the other hand, there has been a 'hyper-politicisation' of grassroots movements (Santos 1994). In several cases, new issues were integrated into party discourse and partisan conflicts have contaminated the life of civic associations. The consequences of this phenomenon were twofold: it limited the autonomy and independence of social mobilisation and it increased the fragmentation and divisions of these groups.

Two examples of this situation can be found in the environmental movement and the mobilisation of women's organisations. First, after the rise of the Partido Ecologista Os Verdes (Green Party, PEV) in the 1980s, the PCP overshadowed the ecological movement, hindering any possibilities to build strong autonomous organisations around this issue (Teixeira 2012). Second, women's movements have remained highly fragmented, politicised and strictly dependent on institutional resources (Ferreira 2011, p. 186).

Despite these structural characteristics, there are significant differences in the relationship the two radical left parties have with social movements. First of all, it is worth emphasising the overlap at the leadership level between the BE and activists of civic organisations and single-issue pressure groups. If we look at the signatures of the founding manifesto (*Começar de novo*), more than ten per cent of supporters at the elite level were activists in NGOs, such as associations for the defence of minorities (women and immigrants) or human rights, or students' associations.[6] Moreover, almost one-third of the founding members participated in trade unions or workers' committees (*comissões de trabalhadores*)[7]. Finally, an important component was associated with the ecologist movement. This was above all the contribution of Política XXI, which inherited specific attention to issues such as sustainable development, the environment and human rights from the MDP (Movimento Democrático Português; see Teixeira 2012).

But it is the distinct approach towards the 'global justice movements' (GJM) that emerged at the beginning of the twenty-first century that most distinguishes the BE from the PCP. It was clear from the outset that the emergence of 'new' social movements depended to a great extent on the role of political parties. Besides participation in the first World Social Forum (WSF) and the European Social Forum (ESF), both parties launched a public debate on the main issues discussed at those meetings, such as trade solidarity, participatory democracy and new social rights. The fact that social movements depended on the initiatives of political parties emerged with the elaboration of the 'Coimbra declaration', a document written in September 2002 that was to represent the launch of the Portuguese Social Forum (PSF). Contrary to what was established at the WSF and ESF, the main social actors accepted the participation of political parties, namely the PCP and the BE (Lima & Nunes 2008). This issue gave rise to the first conflicts among participants. Some civic associations and organisations were against the participation of political parties in the first PSF. In the end, they decided to accept their participation given the strong overlap between party members and civic activists (Nunes 2011).

While the BE was strongly committed to participating in this process in the attempt to establish a stable (but open) relation with social movements, the PCP was more sceptical and less inclined to receiving inputs from civil society. Two aspects are extremely important to understanding this distinct approach: the organisational adaptation and the programmatic orientations. A new position was created in the BE's executive party body which was responsible for dealing with these movements, with the task of supervising their development and finding forms of collaboration, thus aiming to establish a permanent linkage (interview with the BE's organisation secretary). In contrast, the PCP did not undergo any organisational change and the international department managed the relationships with social movements (interview with a member of the PCP's secretariat). The fact that the final document approved during the XVII congress (2004) included only few references to the GJM provides further evidence of the marginal importance of the GJM to the communist leadership.

As for the programmatic dimension, the PCP's emphasis was mainly on its anti-capitalist orientation, defending the nationalisation of strategic sectors—such as energy, transport, banking, industry, communication and media—as well as the intervention of the state in several social and economic domains (Jalali & Lisi 2012). Moreover, the PCP supported traditional social policies, especially those in defence of workers and pensioners' rights, health care and education.

On the other hand, the issues raised with the appearance of the BE have been more consistently new, especially with regard to post-materialist values. Although the involvement of civic organisations in the drafting of party manifesto has remained virtually irrelevant and there were no formal structures to articulate their inputs (with the exception of the 2009 manifesto; see Soeiro 2009), the issues and values associated with the 'global justice movements' constituted an essential component of its identity. Topics such as citizens' rights, the environment, gender equality, racism and trade asymmetries were some of the new subjects that achieved more salience thanks to the BE mobilisation.

A closer look at radical left parties' programmes confirms this picture. Drawing on data from the Comparative Manifesto Project (CMP), we can analyse the salience of post-materialist dimensions for the main Portuguese parties and its evolution over the last decade.[8] Overall, the main findings show that these issues are important for both parties, although on average their salience is higher in the BE's platforms (Figure 1). Although 'new politics' issues also have a relatively high salience for the PCP—especially when compared with the two main governing parties—the BE has clearly showed a more stable commitment to post-materialist orientations, particularly since the 2005 elections. From this viewpoint, these topics can to a great extent be considered the hallmark of the identity of the new left-libertarian party.

These data also seem to indicate a downward trend in the salience of libertarian issues after 2005. This can be explained, at least partially, as the consequence of the demobilisation of GJM following the I PSF. These social movements considered the political parties' influence on the PSF a major weakness. The lack of autonomy and the high level of politicisation of the PSF created significant conflicts within the movement and limited the PSF's scope and its capacity to expand its appeal and to include new social forces.

All in all, the BE approach vis-à-vis social movements was completely different from that of the PCP. While the new party aimed to establish a horizontal and open

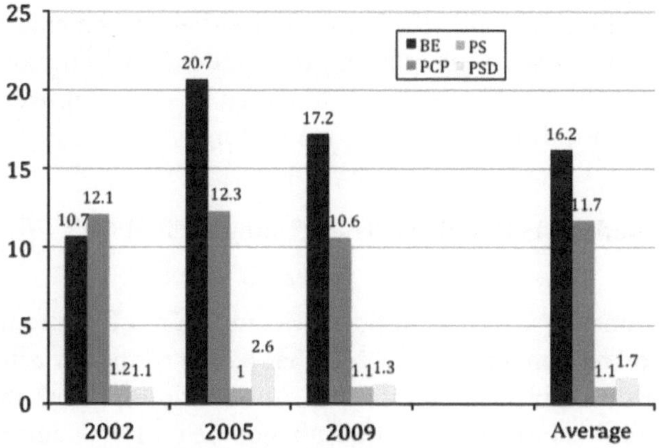

Figure 1 Salience of Post-materialist Issues (2002–09). *Source*: Comparative Manifesto Project (Budge et al. 2001; Klingemann, Volkens & Budge 2006). *Note*: The index includes the following categories: support for peace (P106); environmental protection (P501); negative references to traditional morality (P604); positive references to labour groups (P701); support of underprivileged minority groups (P705); support of non-economic demographic groups (P706).

relationship, the latter was criticised for trying to implement a 'transmission belt' model of linkage. This difference in terms of organisational culture was one of the main problems that the PSF experienced, constraining the mobilisation of social movements. The main trade union confederation (Confederação Geral dos Trabalhadores Portugueses [CGTP]), and especially its leadership, was an important player at that time in order to neutralise the conflicts between the two radical left parties—if not hostility—between the two radical left parties and to mediate their relationship. Moreover, it also played a crucial role in mobilisation and logistic support.

The BE decided not to support the organisation of the II PSF, which became increasingly dominated by the PCP. The communists have always downplayed the autonomous role played by civil society and have considered social movements a temporary and unstable form of mobilisation, inorganic and lacking any real ability to achieve policy change (meeting with the PCP's former secretary of organisation). As for the BE, the decision not to participate in the second edition of the PSF was to create internal conflicts given that the minority—mostly supporters of Ruptura-FER (Frente de Esquerda Revolucionária, Left Revolutionary Front)—criticised the failure (and unwillingness) to mobilise a unified left and to establish a closer relationship with the PCP.[9] This is an example of the party leadership's capacity to adapt to external challenges and to impose its strategic choices. The divisions within the radical left and the increasing politicisation were to determine the collapse of the PSF and the groups associated with the GJM.

Overall, the radical left parties' relationships with social movements presented distinct features. While the BE established wide and relatively strong links with civil society through informal linkages, the PCP maintained more distant, top-down and formal relationships. In other words, the case of the BE can be characterised as a symbiotic relationship and both the party and social movements benefited from mutual collaboration, despite maintaining their autonomy.[10] In contrast, the PCP attempted to influence—but has not been influenced by—social movements, adopting a pragmatic and sceptical stance towards these actors.

The Portuguese Radical Left and the Trade Unions: The PCP's Continuous Dominance

Labour organisations are a second important component of environmental linkage. Since the transition to democracy, the CGTP has remained the key actor in the labour movement. The PCP established a strong and close relationship with the CGTP, which has traditionally been considered the 'transmission belt' of the communists, whereas the UGT (União Geral dos Trabalhadores) has displayed greater autonomy vis-à-vis the main political parties (Morlino 1998; Magone 2001)[11].

In contrast to the communists, the BE had a very marginal presence within the labour movement. Historically, the UDP was the party with the strongest relationship with trade unions—especially in the area south of Lisbon, Santarém and Oporto—while the PSR had some important links within the fishing industries and footwear sector in the north (interview with a member of BE's political commission). Additionally, Ruptura-FER had a very small group of activists within the bank sector.

While the PCP has always been able to maintain its influence on CGTP's orientations, the BE's penetration of the main trade union has been virtually irrelevant.[12] Although CGTP's representatives are usually invited to participate in party conventions, the links are informal and mostly based on personal relationships between top leaders of the two organisations, with no organisational or permanent structures. The presence of BE members within the main trade union confederation has remained weak and limited to specific areas, mainly related to public companies (energy, communication) and the educational sector (teachers and students) (interview with a member of BE's secretariat). From this viewpoint, it is worth noting that one-third of the main body of the party are teachers or university professors (data from the seventh party convention held in 2011).

Given the difficulties of the BE in establishing tighter links with trade unions, the party leadership has given priority to the party's implantation in workers' committees. However, the two 'leftist' components within the party (UDP and Ruptura) have continued to defend the importance of party penetration into the labour movement, as well as more traditional issues related to workers and employment. On the other hand, the PCP has complained about the decline of workers' committees—from almost 500 in 2000 to 350 in 2010 (*O Militante*, January 2011)—and their 'parliamentarisation' due to the reformist orientation of both BE and socialist members.

Data drawn from a national survey of parliamentary candidates conducted in the 2002 and 2009 elections confirm that communists are more strongly anchored to the labour movement, whereas the BE has more differentiated links to civic organisations (Table 1). First, when we look at trade union membership, we find very high integration among communist candidates (60 per cent of communist candidates are also members of a trade union); the socialists showed the weakest anchorage, with the BE occupying an intermediate position (between 37 and 43 per cent). This finding is also confirmed by a recent survey of voters and representatives which found that communist sympathisers are significantly more likely to participate in trade unions than BE militants (Viegas & Santos 2009, pp. 136–137).

Table 1 Membership of MP Candidates within Civic Organisations by Party Affiliation (2002 and 2009)

	Trade unions		Professional associations		Social organis-ations		*N*
	2002	2009	2002	2009	2002	2009	
BE	37.5	43.2	27.1	30.6	32.3	27.0	48–37
PCP	60.3	60.0	27.6	24.0	24.2	26.9	58–25
PS	16.9	24.4	24.2	34.1	37.9	36.6	59–41

Sources: Freire, Viegas & Seiceira (2009); Freire & Viegas (2010).

Second, no significant differences are found among left parties when we look at professional organisations. Approximately one in three of their candidates are also members of a professional organisation, and this percentage has remained relatively stable over the last decade. Third, BE representatives show higher levels of membership in cultural associations, confirming the post-materialist background of the party elites. Fourth, the socialists display higher scores for membership in social organisations, although differences between the left parties are very small. Finally, both radical left parties have an almost negligible percentage of activists involved in religious associations.

Despite the continuous dominance by the PCP of the main trade union, the CGTP leadership has been gaining increasing autonomy vis-à-vis the communists, prompting some dialogue between radical left parties. To a great extent, this may be explained by the authority and respect of the CGTP's secretary-general, Carvalho da Silva. Besides the key role the CGTP played during the PSF, it was also a key actor in fostering the alliance among left forces in support of Manuel Alegre in the 2011 presidential elections. Alegre is a historic socialist leader who, after achieving a much better result in the 2006 presidential elections than the official socialist candidate (Mário Soares), was able to forge a coalition between the PS, the BE and the Communist Renovation—a splinter group from the PCP (Jalali 2012). This experience not only showed the autonomy of the trade union leadership vis-à-vis the PCP, but also the strategic adaptation of the BE leadership in attempting to solve the dilemma between office- and policy-seeking. Ultimately, this attempt to establish some forms of cooperation with the Partido Socialista (PS) and to dissociate itself from the communists is another important factor that explains BE's poor performance in the 2011 legislative elections.

Overall, the relationship between radical left parties and trade unions has been characterised by huge asymmetry. The PCP has maintained a strong presence (and control) within the labour movement, while the role played by the BE has been marginal. Although the left-libertarian party has tried to strengthen its links with trade unions, no significant changes can be observed in terms of environmental linkages. First, the party has preserved informal relationships at the leadership level and a weak penetration of grassroots structures. Second, the competition between the two radical left parties within labour organisations, as well as the presence of radical factions, led the BE to give more emphasis to traditional social policies while continuing to own post-materialist issues. Thus, both the organisational legacy and the competitive challenges have influenced environmental linkages and the strategy of mobilisation of radical left parties.

The Portuguese Radical Left and the Economic Crisis

With the economic and financial crisis that emerged in 2008, Portugal experienced a wave of intense mobilisation led by the main trade union confederation and radical left parties. In the early months of 2010 both the BE and the PCP supported several demonstrations against the public sector cuts (transportation, health and education) implemented by the socialist government. The mobilisation intensified when the government presented the 2011 state budget, leading to several protests from public employees and a general strike that took place in November 2010. Once again, the CGTP played an important role in fostering a united front among radical left parties.

While both the PCP and the BE supported these traditional forms of mobilisation, they adopted different stances towards the new movements that emerged after the economic crisis. Precarious employment was the main issue behind this new kind of mobilisation. After the first Mayday held in 2007, some new movements emerged focusing on employment-related issues (especially autonomous jobs), social security and public services. The BE played a crucial role in fostering the mobilisation of these new movements,[13] encouraging and supporting their action in several ways. In contrast, the PCP adopted a more critical position, showing its scepticism about the cohesion of this form of mobilisation and its impact on the political system. According to the party leadership, this kind of protest is based on a heterogeneous movement with no 'class consciousness' and no clear objectives, whose importance and growth were inflated by the mass media and opinion-makers (interview with a member of PCP's secretariat). Consequently, they regard these movements as a short-term form of mobilisation with little chance of influencing the austerity measures implemented under the loan agreement established in May 2011.[14]

The BE's active role is visible through its organisational support, programmatic influence and leadership overlap. First, the BE participated in several of these movements' initiatives by offering logistic and material support, especially through the participation of a large portion of its activists. Second, the BE had a crucial impact on the elaboration of the platforms of some of these new movements. True, the problem of precarious jobs has been a constant in its programmatic platforms.[15] Yet the BE played an important role in articulating such issues, through the drafting of specific proposals, as well as taking an intermediation role in the parliamentary arena. As a consequence, these single-issue groups have been quite active in legislative bill proposals. Finally, some of the members included in the main national party bodies also belong to the leadership of these associations. This overlap is even more marked when we consider activists at lower echelons.

This new type of single-issue group is still somewhat incipient. They have very limited resources in terms of personnel and funding, their action mobilises only specific sectors and they find it difficult to articulate their particular demands into a broader platform (interview with social movement activist). Despite this, these movements have enjoyed high visibility in public opinion, achieving a peak of mobilisation with the huge demonstration held in March 2011 when more than 300,000 people rallied against both the political and the economic crisis. The novelty of this mobilisation was that political parties did not take part in organising the protest. In other words, it was a form of spontaneous and non-partisan mobilisation that was organised through the internet and the use of social networks.

The BE strategy was to politicise this issue by campaigning in support of these causes. Accordingly, as early as February 2011 the BE launched a campaign with the slogan 'precariousness is not the future' on small advertising billboards. These themes were developed in the campaign with explicit references to the 'struggling generation' (*geração à rasca*) in TV spots, with a series of short announcements each dealing with a different professional or social group. This issue was also connected to the lack of representation of the young and the unresponsiveness of the main political parties, thus reinforcing the argument against the 'cartelisation' of the political system.

The relationship between these forms of mobilisation and radical left parties has been characterised in terms of loose and weak linkages. Many civic organisations are strongly non-partisan—even anti-party—and aim to maintain their autonomy in order to reach a broader audience. The BE has clearly supported this form of mobilisation by joining their demonstrations and articulating their main concerns. The aim of this strategy was not only to widen the BE social base—especially young and disaffected citizens—but also to link traditional economic and social issues to post-materialist values. The PCP has adopted a less enthusiastic position, giving priority to the traditional mobilisation of trade unions rather than to spontaneous forms of political participation. Yet both parties have tried to represent their concerns at the institutional level by actively presenting bill proposals against precarious jobs, articulating the demands of social movements.

Although it is too early to examine the role of these new forms of mobilisation, popular discontent has displayed relatively low salience despite the strong austerity measures implemented by the Portuguese government. This new situation has affected the BE, while the PCP has proved to be relatively immune. In particular, the BE's electoral defeat at the 2011 legislative election and its unsuccessful strategy of mobilisation have triggered internal criticism within the party. As a consequence, the party has undertaken a debate on both the generational turnover at the elite level and also the leadership model that would best share power among the several factions. After internal criticism, Louçã announced his withdrawal from the party leadership and proposed a dual leadership to be elected at the eighth party convention in November 2012. This should allow the representation of the main internal factions, as well as the rise of younger generations with more links to social movements.

Conclusions

This paper has examined the relationship of Portuguese radical left parties with civil society, focusing on participatory and environmental linkages. The objectives of this study are twofold: firstly, to analyse the strength and breadth of these ties and whether they have changed over the last two decades; secondly, to address factors that may explain these kinds of linkage.

My first finding indicates that the two radical left parties established different ties with civil society. In terms of participatory linkages, the PCP has followed the traditional Leninist party model with strong vertical links, a tight encapsulation of party members and a high level of institutionalisation. Despite internal pressure for change, participatory linkages have remained unchanged with no greater openness or inclusiveness of grassroots structures. This contrasts with the features displayed by the BE's organisational model. Not only have decision-making processes emphasised members' participation, but also leadership–members relations have been less articulated, displaying a very low level of institutionalisation. In practice, however, the mobilisation of members has proved to be increasingly difficult and there has been a growing centralisation over the last decade.

Moving to the environmental dimension, the PCP has had a top-down relation with ancillary organisations. By contrast, the BE established a more open and symbiotic relationship with social organisations, with close links especially to civic rights associations. Moreover, while the contacts between the BE and civil society remained informal, the PCP aimed to establish an organic link through party structures. As far as the BE is concerned, the rise of GJM had two important effects: on the one hand, it increased the overlap between the party and social movements at both the leadership and grassroots level; on the other, the range of relations widened. Overall, these results substantially confirmed our main hypotheses regarding the impact of organisational models on the type of linkages established by radical left parties.

The communists have always privileged their relationship with trade unions, whereas support for social movements was mainly strategic due to the competition with the BE and the expected gains in terms of electoral performance. On the other hand, the new left-libertarian party has changed the type of linkage with civic associations, fostering more autonomous relations and more pragmatic alliances with specific groups based on 'precarious jobs' movements. Several factors help explain this adaptation. First, following the 2005 elections in particular, the BE went through a process of institutionalisation and increasing centralisation which granted the dominant coalition greater autonomy vis-à-vis the rank and file. This has allowed the party leadership to give more attention to the institutional and strategic component. Second, the demobilisation of the GJM and the economic crisis have led to a redefinition of the BE's mobilisation strategy towards more traditional forms of protest, in terms of both content and form. Finally, the socialist government implemented several civic rights policies (abortion, divorce, same sex marriage) that have favoured this adaptation process. But the important thing to note is that the type of party linkage adopted by both parties was instrumental to the strategic challenges of party competition. From this viewpoint, the electoral arena made party leaders take crucial decisions in order to improve their party's electoral success.

The second main finding suggests that the relationship between radical left parties and civil society depends on both external and internal factors. As far as the first aspect is concerned, the strategy of mobilisation of both parties was linked to the politics of alliance and to electoral pressures. More important, however, was the role played by internal factors. As other Western countries have shown, divergences within the left in terms of organisational and programmatic characteristics are important to explain how issues raised by these groups are channelled inside the institutions (Andretta &

Reiter 2009). The genetic model had a significant impact on the type of linkage between radical left parties and civil society. Moreover, the legacy and strength of traditional links with civic organisations determined the different mobilisation strategy. Finally, in the case of the BE, intra-party conflicts also help explain the difficulty of defining a coherent strategy, as well as its pragmatic orientation after 2005.

Overall, this study emphasises two important aspects of the relationship between radical left parties and civil society. The first is that party organisation matters. This does not mean that there is a determinist relationship between party types and mobilisation strategy. This relationship is always mediated by party leadership and the dynamics of party competition. This strategic component emerges when we consider the need to combine social mobilisation with institutional integration. As the Portuguese case shows, radical left parties attempt to resolve this dilemma through an adaptation process. The second important implication of this study is that there is a mutual interest in establishing some forms of linkages between radical left parties and civil society. On the one hand, both the PCP and the BE consider civic organisations an important asset for electoral and social mobilisation; moreover, participatory and environmental linkages also play an important role in terms of legitimacy. On the other, given the structural weakness of civil society, social movements and organised associations need to establish links with radical left parties in order to receive organisational support and to articulate their demands in the institutional arena. Notwithstanding this, the impact of civil society on radical left parties has been very limited both in terms of programmatic and organisational characteristics and also with regard to the degree of participation and the improvement of representative channels.

Notes

[1] In 2000, the BE included also the fourth component, Ruptura-FER (Left Revolutionary Front), an extreme left-wing group which is the Portuguese representative of the International Workers League (Fourth International).

[2] See the interview with Miguel Portas, *Expresso*, 14 October 2000. In particular, the mobilisation of civil society for the first referendum on abortion in 1998 and the demonstrations in defence of East Timor's independence played a crucial role in the emergence of this new political party.

[3] Like other left-libertarian parties, the BE has adopted the rule of MP rotation. However, it has been increasingly difficult for the party to respect this criterion due to the expansion of its parliamentary group as shown by the strong continuity of the main party leaders.

[4] See, among others, the recent document 'O Bloco e os caminhos da Esquerda' elaborated after the electoral defeat in 2011.

[5] Since the IV convention in 2005, several criticisms have emerged with regard to the oligarchic character of party structures, the routinisation of internal procedures, and the lack of information for the majority of party members. See, for example, motion B ('Por uma Plataforma de Democracia Socialista') presented at the 2005 party meeting. The same document was also presented at the 2007 convention. These criticisms were also made at the 2011 convention, emphasising the need to strengthen openness and the renovation of the party.

[6] This reflects what happened for green parties, where the first generation of party elites had previous political experience as activists in social movements (Poguntke 2006).

[7] Workers' committees are institutions that aim to represent workers in their relationships with companies. These structures emerged during the democratic transition and opposed the attempt of the CGTP and PCP to control the labour movement. They developed strong links with extreme-left parties and displayed more radical orientations.

[8] I created an index of left-libertarian orientations which includes the following items: peace, environmental protection, negative references to traditional morality, positive references to labour and non-economic demographic groups (i.e. women, old people, young people, linguistic groups, etc.), and support of underprivileged minority groups..

[9] See the document 'O Rumo Estratégico do Bloco' elaborated after the 2005 elections.

[10] There is a symbiotic relationship when one actor is dependent on the other and vice versa. Traditionally, this kind of phenomenon is seen in the relationship between Catholic parties and religious associations (Morlino 1998; Thomas 2001).

[11] The UGT was formed in the 1970s with the support of the two main parties (PS and Partido Social Democrata [PSD]) and played a marginal role in the mobilisation of workers' movements, giving priority to the development of institutional relations with the government.

[12] The PSR only elected its first representative in the CGTP in 1993. However, during the last decade the BE was not represented on the main executive board.

[13] Some of the most active groups close to the BE include associations of independent or precarious jobs (FERVE—*Fartas/os d'Estes Recibos Verdes, Precarious inflexíveis*), or performing artists (Intermitentes do espectáculo).

[14] Due to the deterioration of the economic and financial situation, the socialist government was forced to ask for a bailout which then led the so-called troika (International Monetary Fund [IMF], European Central Bank [ECB], European Commission [EC]) to set out significant austerity measures and a plan of structural reforms.

[15] References to precarious work were also present in the 2002 and 2005 electoral manifestos. However, it was mainly related to specific groups such as immigrants or part-time jobs.

References

Allern, E. H. (2010) *Political Parties and Interest Groups in Norway*, ECPR Press, London.

Allern, E. H. & Bale, T. (2012) 'Political parties and interest groups: disentangling complex relationships', *Party Politics*, vol. 18, no. 1, pp. 7–25.

Andretta, M. & Reiter, H. (2009) 'Parties, unions and movements. The European left and the ESF', in *Another Europe: Conceptions and Practices of Democracy in the European Social Forums*, ed. D. Della Porta, Routledge, London, pp. 173–203.

Bosco, A. (2001) 'Four actors in search of a role: the Southern European communist parties', in *Parties, Politics, and Democracy in the New Southern Europe*, eds P. N. Diamandouros & R. Gunther, Johns Hopkins University Press, Baltimore, pp. 329–387.

Budge, I., Klingemann, H.-D., Volkens, A., Bara, J. & Tanenbaum, E. (2001) *Mapping Policy Preferences*, Oxford University Press, Oxford.

Caul Kittilson, M. & Scarrow, S. E. (2003) 'Political parties and the rhetoric and realities of democratization', in *Democracy Transformed? Expanding Political Opportunities in Advanced Industrial Democracies*, eds B. E. Cain, R. J. Dalton & S. E. Scarrow, Oxford University Press, Oxford, pp. 59–80.

Cruz, M. Bragada (1995) *Instituições Políticas e Processos Sociais*, Bertrand, Lisboa.

Cunha, C. (1992) *The Portuguese Communist Party's Strategy for Power, 1921–1986*, Garland, New York.

Dunphy, R. & Bale, T. (2011) 'The radical left in coalition government: towards a comparative measurement of success and failure', *Party Politics*, vol. 17, no. 4, pp. 488–504.

Ferreira, V. (2011) 'Engendering Portugal: social change, state politics and women's social mobilization', in *Contemporary Portugal*, ed. A. C. Pinto, Social Science Monograph, New York, pp. 153–192.

Freire, A. & Viegas, J. M. L. (eds) (2010) 'Inquérito aos candidatos a deputados – Legislativas de 2009 – Base de Dados', data set elaborated within the project 'Os Deputados Portugueses em Perspectiva Comparada: Eleições, Liderança e Representação Política' (PTDC/CPO/64469/2006), 2008–2010, ISCTE, CIES-IUL, Lisboa.

Freire, A., Viegas, J. M. L. & Seiceira, F. (eds) (2009) *A Representação Política em Portugal – Inquéritos e Bases de Dados*, Sextante, Lisboa.

Jalali, C. (2007) *Partidos e Democracia em Portugal 1974–2005*, Imprensa de Ciências Sociais, Lisboa.

Jalali, C. (2012) 'The 2011 Portuguese presidential elections: incumbency advantage in semi–presidentialism?', *South European Society and Politics*, vol. 17, no. 2, pp. 239–260.

Jalali, C. & Lisi, M. (2012) 'Quand le changement semble dangereux: l'évolution du Parti communiste portugais', in *Les partis de la gauche anticapitaliste en Europe*, eds J. -M. De Waele & D. -L. Seiler, Economica, Paris, pp. 180–204.

Katz, R. S. (1990) 'Party as linkage: a vestigial function?', *European Journal of Political Research*, vol. 18, no. 1, pp. 143–161.

Katz, R. S. & Mair, P. (1995) 'Changing models of party organization and party democracy: the emergence of the cartel party', *Party Politics*, vol. 1, no. 1, pp. 5–28.

Kitschelt, H. (1988) 'Left-libertarian parties: explaining innovation in competitive party systems', *World Politics*, vol. 40, no. 2, pp. 194–234.

Kitschelt, H. (2006) 'Movement parties', in *Handbook of Party Politics*, eds R. S. Katz & W. J. Crotty, Sage, London, pp. 278–290.

Klingemann, H. -D., Volkens, A. & Budge, I. (eds) (2006) *Mapping Policy Preferences II*, Oxford University Press, Oxford.

Lima, M. Piresde & Nunes, C. (2008) 'Portogallo: il caso della creazione del Forum Sociale portoghese', in *Europa Alterglobal. Componenti e culture del 'Movimento dei Movimenti' in Europa*, eds A. Farro & P. Rebughini, Franco Angeli, Milano, pp. 176–186.

Lisi, M. (2009) 'New politics in Portugal: the rise and success of the Left Bloc', *Pôle Sud*, vol. 30, no. 1, pp. 127–144.

Lisi, M. (2011) *Os Partidos Políticos em Portugal: Continuidade e Transformação*, Almedina, Coimbra.

Magone, J. M. (2001) *Iberian Trade Unionism*, Transaction, New Brunswick, NJ.

March, L. (2011) *Radical Left Parties in Contemporary Democracies*, Routledge, London.

McDonnell, D. & Newell, J. (2011) 'Outsider parties in government in Western Europe', *Party Politics*, vol. 17, no. 4, pp. 443–452.

Morlino, L. (1998) *Democracy between Consolidation and Crisis*, Oxford University Press, Oxford.

Nunes, C. (2011) 'Expressões alterglobais na sociedade portuguesa: ecos transnacionais de novas formas de acção colectiva?', CIES e-working paper, ISCTE-IUL, Lisboa.

Panebianco, A. (1988) *Political Parties. Organisation and Power*, Oxford University Press, Oxford.

Poguntke, T. (2002) 'Party organizational linkage: parties without firm social roots?', in *Political Parties in the New Europe*, eds K. R. Luther & F. Müller-Rommel, Oxford University Press, Oxford, pp. 43–62.

Poguntke, T. (2006) 'Political parties and other organizations', in *Handbook of Party Politics*, eds R. S. Katz & W. J. Crotty, Sage, London, pp. 396–405.

Santos, B. de Sousa (1994) *Pela mão de Alice: o social e o político na pós-modernidade*, Afrontamento, Porto.

Sartori, G. (2005) 'Party types, organisation and functions', *West European Politics*, vol. 28, no. 1, pp. 5–32.

Schattschneider, E. E. (1942) *Party Government*, Greenwood Press, New York.

Selle, P. (1997) 'Parties and voluntary organizations: strong or weak ties?', in *Challenges to Political Parties: The Case of Norway*, eds K. Strøm & L. Svåsand, University of Michigan Press, Ann Arbor, pp. 149–166.

Soeiro, J. (2009) 'The "Bloco de Esquerda" and the founding of a new left in Portugal', in *The Left in Europe*, eds C. Hildebrandt & B. Daiber, Rosa Luxemburg Foundation, Brussels, pp. 176–183.

Teixeira, L. H. (2012) *Verdes Anos. História do ecologismo em Portugal*, Esfera do Caos, Lisboa.

Thomas, C. S. (ed.) (2001) *Political Parties and Interest Groups: Shaping Democratic Governance*, Lynne Rienner, Boulder.

Viegas, J. M. L. & Santos, S. (2009) 'Envolvimento dos cidadãos e dos parlamentares nas associações', in *A Representação Política. O Caso Português em Perspectiva Comparada*, eds A. Freire & J. M. L. Viegas, Sextante, Lisboa, pp. 119–143.

Viegas, J. M. L., Faria, S. & Santos, S. (2010) 'Envolvimento associativo e mobilização cívica', in *A qualidade da democracia em debate*, eds J. M. L. Viegas, S. Santos & S. Faria, Mundos Sociais, Lisboa, pp. 157–180.

Marco Lisi is an Assistant Professor in the Department of Political Studies, Universidade Nova of Lisbon. He has published two books on Portuguese political parties and several articles on political parties and electoral behaviour in international journals such as *West European Politics*, *South European Society and Politics* and *Representation*.

Impulse and Decadence of Linkage Processes: Evidence from the Spanish Radical Left

Luis Ramiro and Tània Verge

Reacting to a profound electoral and organisational crisis, in the mid-1980s the Communist Party of Spain initiated a process of party change which envisioned empowering members in decision-making processes and establishing closer and wider relations with civil society. Party change eventually led to the creation of a new organisation, United Left. This article gives an account of the design and implementation of participatory and environmental linkages by the Spanish United Left and evaluates their specific outputs. We show that United Left's strategies aimed at reinvigorating linkage have had very limited success, failing to stabilise the party's electoral fortunes, to reconnect with society and to expand its membership.

Contemporary debates over the representational functions of political parties tend to be dominated by the assumption that they have detached themselves from social groups and have no interest in forging more than tenuous links with society—among other reasons because they can comfortably rely on public funding. Indeed, an active membership and party–group linkages could be even considered as obstacles for flexible and electoral market-oriented parties (Katz & Mair 1995). This notwithstanding, daily party practices escape simple assimilation to the more 'ideal-type' versions of the electoral-professional and catch-all parties (Poguntke 2002; Thomas 2001; Yishai 2001). Parties are found to still seek connection with social groups (Allern 2010). The need for legitimacy and the increasing public demands for a more participatory democracy might counterbalance the influences towards the loss of importance of members for parties (Dalton & Wattenberg 2000; Kitschelt 1994, p. 299). Similarly, selective incentives that empower party members might also help parties compensate for the erosion of their capacity to deliver solidarity incentives (Scarrow, Webb & Farrell 2000).

While the move that makes parties more distant from society has been widely exposed, the strategy that attempts to rebuild linkages is far less studied (Allern & Bale 2012). However, in the era of electoral-professional parties, some parties have undertaken considerable organisational changes in order to strengthen the linkage process. Western communist parties are an interesting example of party change and, particularly, of the strategies aimed at reconstructing linkage. Their strong attachment to the mass party model with regard to members' role and internal procedures as well as their lack of financial means to run professional and expensive campaigns suggest they cannot be affected in the same way as other parties by the trend towards the dismissal of party members' relevance. Besides, both the discourse and the organisational strategies of communist parties have traditionally emphasised the representational function of the party and its need to be in close contact with its social milieu. Therefore, party–group linkages and active party members are expected to be more valued than in other party families. Simultaneously, communist parties have faced pressing environmental challenges such as cultural and social changes adverse to party identity, an acute ideological crisis, a massive loss of party members, and a remarkable electoral decline (Waller & Fennema 1988; Bell 1993; Bull & Heywood 1994; Bosco 2000; Botella & Ramiro 2003), which have called for urgent action to rebuild their organisational and electoral appeal.

Accordingly, we could expect communist parties to have changed their strategies towards linkage processes, although in a limited way. They are expected to modify both candidate and leadership selection and policy-making procedures towards greater involvement of party members while elite monitoring is safeguarded through the control of these processes by conventional party organs—something favoured by the parties' traditional and rigid organisational principles. Regarding social organisations, efforts to rebuild linkage are expected to stem from both the process of ideological renewal through which some communist parties have recently adopted new politics issues, including participatory democracy ideals, and the need to redesign their electoral bases of support.

This article aims to describe and evaluate the design, implementation and specific outputs of the two components of the linkage process by the Spanish radical left throughout the 1980s to the 2010s, namely 'participatory linkage', consisting of channelling the involvement of individual party members in the party's decision-making process, and 'environmental linkage', dealing with interest representation and, more specifically, establishing diverse links with organised civil society (Lawson 1980; Merkl 2005; Schwartz 2005). Analysis of the Spanish communists, whose leaders explicitly embraced strategies to strengthen linkage, allows us to uncover which factors may foster this strategy and to determine the extent to which it has been successful. This wide time frame allows us to evaluate these strategies (and the forms of linkage developed) in a more informative way so as to better capture variation over time and discuss party changes against the broader organisational dynamics and electoral trends the Spanish radical left has experienced over the past few decades.

In the mid-1980s, in reaction to electoral failure and internal crisis, the leadership of the Partido Comunista de España (Communist Party of Spain, PCE) decided to design a new political and organisational strategy. The communists began a process of party change through a plan to create a new organisation, Izquierda Unida (United Left, IU), in the development of which the PCE would have a key role (Ramiro 2004a). The organisational dimension involved according this new party more democratic internal functioning than traditional parties. In this vein, communist leaders stressed the importance of participatory linkage, granting the rank and file more influence in decision-making processes. The political dimension included establishing closer and wider relations with civil society, opening the traditional left towards a more intense relationship with a broad range of social groups and thereby stressing the relevance of environmental linkage.

The remainder of the article is organised as follows. The second section presents the PCE's and IU's electoral and membership evolution with some notes on recurrent problems with factional strife. The third section explores the design and implementation of the parties' linkage strategies over the past three decades. The concluding section assesses party change in relation to the two types of linkage under study and evaluates their degree of success in attaining broader party goals.

The PCE and the IU

The PCE was unable to capitalise on its role as the main opposition party under dictatorship rule and obtained just 9.3 per cent of the vote in the first democratic elections. By 1982 the party's electoral support had more than halved (see Table 1). In the mid-1980s the PCE began working with other minor left parties to ultimately form the IU coalition in 1986 as a means to counteract the electoral crisis of communism by launching an organisation whose platform would add new politics issues, such as feminist and environmental demands, to the traditional concerns of the left. Although plans were initially made to dissolve the founding parties into IU, the PCE maintained a prominent role in the new organisation and preserved a traditional radical left identity for IU. In the early 1990s the original electoral coalition model was abandoned through internal reforms that unified the organisation of IU. However, despite recurrent debates, the communist leadership did not dissolve the PCE into the new organisation. Since the mid-2000s the PCE has been the only relevant party to remain in IU, the rest having gradually abandoned it after frequent internal strife.[1] The PCE has always been the most important actor within IU and many of its activists are IU cadres.

Disputes about strategies towards the Partido Socialista Obrero Español (Spanish Socialist Workers' Party, PSOE) and towards the unions, and disagreements about the ideological and organisational definition of IU have made the party's internal life particularly conflictual. Besides, IU's permissiveness towards dissent is entrenched in

Table 1 PCE's and IU's Electoral Results, 1977–2011

	PCE (1977–1982)			IU (1986–2011)							
Legislative elections*	1977	1979	1982	1986	1989	1993	1996	2000	2004	2008	2011
Votes (%)	9.3	10.8	4.0	4.6	9.1	9.5	10.5	5.4	4.9	3.8	6.9
Seats (*N*)	19	23	4	7	17	18	21	8	3†	1†	9‡
Regional elections			*1983*	*1987*	*1991*	*1995*	*1999*	*2003*	*2007*		*2011*
Votes (%)			7.6	6.7	9.4	10.8	5.2	5.9	6.1		5.2
Seats (*N*)			52	46	74	97	36	48	47		51
Local elections		*1979*	*1983*	*1987*	*1991*	*1995*	*1999*	*2003*	*2007*		*2011*
Votes (%)		12.7	8.0	7.2	8.4	11.7	6.5	6.1	5.5		6.3
Seats (*N*)		3,608	2,495	2,641	2,614	3,493	2,295	2,198	2,034		2,230

Source: Spanish Ministry of Interior and www.historiaelectoral.com

*Congress of Deputies, 350 seats.

†The percentage of votes includes those obtained by its coalition partner in Catalonia, Iniciativa per Catalunya Verds, which obtained two seats in 2004, one seat in 2008 and two seats in 2011, which are not added to the total count of IU seats in the table.

‡Excluding coalition partners.

party statutes due to the need to accommodate the ideologically diverse groups that formed IU in conjunction with the PCE (communists of several tendencies, left socialists, republicans, environmentalists and feminists, among others). IU allows the creation of factions and even parties, which are allowed to present their candidates in internal elections. Seats in decision-making bodies are allocated among the competing lists obtaining at least ten per cent of the delegates' vote in the party conference, which tends to produce divided dominant coalitions. The faction system has not been peaceful at all, open conflict leading to expulsions, splits and members' defections (Paniagua & Ramiro 2003; Verge & Gómez 2012).

IU experienced a significant gain in votes from the mid-1980s to the mid-1990s, reaching its peak in 1996 (10.5 per cent of the national vote). Since then it suffered a dramatic and steady electoral decline until 2011, albeit maintaining itself as the third most popular national party (see Table 1). Whereas IU had typically attracted disaffected socialist voters, once the PSOE became an opposition party in 1996 IU not only stopped receiving an inflow of socialist voters, but also started suffering a significant decrease in its own vote share. In 2008 its presence at the Congress of Deputies was reduced to one seat and it became an extra-parliamentary force in six of the 17 regional parliaments while maintaining a very weak presence in the others. The progressive loss of national and regional deputies was aggravated by the significant reduction in the number of local councillors, which only stopped at the 2011 general, regional and local elections due to the major backlash suffered by the PSOE. Yet IU's increase was modest. At the national level, whereas the PSOE lost 59 seats the IU only gained eight seats, and at the regional level the increase was even more marginal.

As Table 2 shows, both the PCE and IU have suffered a continuous outflow of members. IU has been recurrently concerned about its low membership levels (Méndez, Morales & Ramiro 2004), although recruitment campaigns launched at the national and regional levels in the mid-1990s were never well planned or well funded, these efforts being more rhetorical than real. In 2004 the party conference mandated the implementation of a new affiliation campaign, which the intense factional infighting the organisation was going through rendered ineffective (Verge 2007, p. 135). Indeed, in the period 2004–08 IU lost about 18,000 members, reaching the membership levels typical of the late 1980s. In any case, this concern about membership recruitment has gone hand in hand with the permanent inaccuracy of IU membership records, particularly in some regional federations, which successive national leaderships have proved unable to fix until 2012.

Severe electoral defeats have brought change in IU's national leadership. The disastrous results in the 1999 local and European elections and in the 2000 legislative elections encouraged the new leadership to seek to de-radicalise the party's discourse by re-launching the organisation as a post-communist eco-socialist party (Verge 2010, p. 90). At the party conference held in 2000, the two contending candidates for the position of party leader belonged to the inner circles of the PCE and IU leadership groups: Gaspar Llamazares, the leader of the IU and PCE regional federation of Asturias, and Francisco Frutos, PCE's secretary-general. Llamazares was elected with

Table 2 PCE and IU Party Membership, 1975–2012

Party	Year	Total	M/E	M/V
PCE	1975	15,000	–	–
	1977	201,740	0.86	11.76
	1979	168,100	0.63	8.67
	1982	181,950	0.68	21.49
IU	1986	70,000	0.24	7.48
	1989	49,730	0.17	2.67
	1993	57,303	0.18	2.54
	1996	65,099	0.20	2.47
	2000	65,000	0.19	5.15
	2004	67,802	0.20	5.28
	2008	50,801	0.14	5.23
	2012	30,000	0.08	1.77

Source: Own elaboration based on Ramiro (2000, p. 257) and Verge (2007, p. 113). Data for 2008 correspond to the membership census used for the organisation of the party conference in 2009. Data for 2012: personal communication with party officials. The decrease in IU membership in 2012 is due to a process of regularisation and centralisation of the membership files which showed that the number of paying members was much lower than the regional party branches had previously reported.
Note: M/E: ratio of members/(Spanish) electorate; M/V: ratio of members/(PCE/IU) voters.

only one more vote than his rival, and was thus forced to integrate members of the losing faction into the party directorate. This election interrupted a long-established tradition by which PCE's secretary-general was also IU's leader. Since then, and until 2008, the PCE leadership acted as an opposition faction within IU's dominant coalition.

The 2008 electoral results forced Llamazares to resign as party leader. Subsequently, he was replaced by the candidate of the PCE's most critical faction, led by Cayo Lara, who urged the party to distance itself from the PSOE (in national government from 2004 until 2011) and stepped up a rhetoric of radicalisation (see Verge 2010, p. 101). Yet, the national leadership still has a heterogeneous composition.

Design and Implementation of Party Linkage

Throughout the last 25 years the electoral performance of IU—the organisation under which the PCE has run in elections since 1986—has experienced ups and downs and, simultaneously, the strategies of empowering party members ('participatory linkage') and reinforcing linkages with the party's social milieu ('environmental linkage') have also gone through phases of impulse and decadence. Regarding participatory linkage, our analysis focuses on the opportunities for members' participation in candidate and leader selection as well as in policy-making. Concerning environmental linkage, we concentrate on the relationships established with organised civil society, as well as the underlying rationale.

Participatory Linkage

Strengthening the role of party members and empowering them became one of the main themes of the party's internal discourse when IU began to develop its own organisation beyond the initial electoral coalition. IU's first party conferences (1989 and 1990) assumed as guiding principles the promotion to the fullest extent of citizens' involvement in the party (including elaborating the party programme), and the designing of local organisations open to the widest participation of members and sympathisers. IU aimed at organisationally recreating the model of participatory democracy that its party manifestos claimed to bring to society at large. Both leaders and party documents argued that IU's new politics required a more open, more democratic and more participatory organisation. The opposition between the 'old politics' of traditional parties and the 'new politics' advocated by IU, at both the ideological and the organisational levels, is constant in party documents during the late 1980s and early 1990s. According to party leaders, IU was to be a 'social and political movement', a new type of participatory organisation open to the involvement of members, non-members and civil society groups. The extension of participatory linkage was also believed to be instrumental in stopping membership decline and in attracting new affiliates. However, as shown below, actual practice has fallen very short of the original purposes in three areas in which members' empowerment might be more visible, namely candidate selection, leader selection and policy-making.

Candidate selection. In 1992 IU formulated the possibility of organising closed party primaries (only members are entitled to participate) for the selection of electoral candidates. Nonetheless, most local party branches have so few members that a sort of general assembly is routinely used for the selection of local candidates. Regarding the selection of candidates for other layers of government, the picture is more complex. For national legislative elections, in spite of the official discourse favourable to participatory politics, this procedure is only vaguely mentioned in party documents. Primaries are neither the compulsory nor the sole procedure for candidate selection. Although primaries should have an undefined 'priority' when more than one candidate competes, there is no single, general and undisputed regulation, and membership ballot results are to be approved by the Federal (namely, national) Executive Committee.

In practice, the use of primaries has been very infrequent and mainly found at the regional level, although there is not even a consistent pattern in the regional branches that have applied them. Primaries may be used in one election while other less inclusive methods are chosen for subsequent elections.[2] It should be noted that the use of primaries has always been surrounded by conflict and strife. For example, in the regional branch of Madrid, a district where in spite of the electoral crisis IU has always elected representatives, primaries were held in 1993 and 1996 to select the national parliamentary candidates (except the head of the list, who is by default the party's candidate for prime minister, already nominated by the Federal Executive

Committee). In 1993, once the primaries had been held, both the process and the results were contested by a faction of the regional executive committee, the latter imposing a new vote and managing to have the order of the list modified—the reason being that this faction had more weight within the regional executive committee than among grassroots members. In 1996, communist members were 'invited' to vote in favour of the candidates supported by the PCE. This sort of informal and non-regulated campaign to influence members' vote was understood by non-PCE factions as a means through which the PCE tried to subtly impose its hegemony on IU's electoral ticket against the principles of pluralism and consensus promoted by the party statutes. After these turbulent experiences, primaries were not used in the subsequent national legislative elections, while the national leadership did not show any intention at all of promoting their use.

So, in contrast to the party's discourse and even the evolution of other contemporary parties, the use of primaries is far from consolidated and institutionalised in IU. The link between internal conflict and primaries is one of the main features of the use of this procedure in IU. Primaries are the last resort when inter-factional agreement cannot be reached through other informal practices. They are not generally promoted by the leadership and their use is subject to the calculus of the different factions to determine which selection procedure is more advantageous to them (namely, primaries or selection by the Federal Executive Committee). This can be well exemplified by the only occasion IU has used primaries to select its candidate for prime minister. In the months before the 2008 national legislative elections, amidst an internal climate of strong division on the party's political strategy, the PCE leadership instigated the use of primaries in order to prevent the nomination of the IU leader, Llamazares, as candidate for prime minister. The PCE launched an alternative candidacy, that of Marga Sanz, who was the leader of the PCE in the Valencia region. Llamazares accepted the challenge and obtained 62.5 per cent of the members' votes. Subsequently his faction tried to take advantage of this victory to extend the use of primaries for the selection of candidates' tickets at the constituency level, with a view to ensuring that IU's parliamentary group would lean towards Llamazares. However, the PCE changed its mind on primaries and made use of its majority in the executive committees of some regions to nominate candidates without primaries. This new internal confrontation was the origin of an acute crisis. Primaries were used at the provincial level in two key electoral districts, specifically in Valencia and Sevilla, and entailed episodes of severe strife. The results were eventually modified by the Valencian and Andalusian regional executive committees, respectively. As a result, the regional branch of IU in Valencia split.

Even if some factions demonstrate their discomfort with this state of affairs, it is clear that the majority of the organisation has not adopted primaries as a party routine. Not even during the period in which the electoral decline endangered the survival of IU, in the aftermath of the 2008 elections, did the party adopt more inclusive methods of candidate selection. Cadres' mistrust of open primaries (open to non-members) and the vague definition of the procedure have rendered them an exceptional event in IU. When they have taken place, it has always been at the local level, in some cases against the will of the national leadership (selection of the candidate to mayor of Jaén in the 2007 local elections), and in others tolerated by it (selection of the candidate to mayor of Valladolid in the 2011 local elections).[3]

Party leader selection. The procedure for the selection of the party leader has remained basically unchanged over time and no relevant innovations have been introduced to increase members' involvement. The election of IU's leader is a two-step indirect process. During the national party conference, party delegates select half the members of the highest party board, namely the Federal Political Committee, who will thereafter choose the party leader in a separate vote. The distribution of offices in this party board is proportional to the votes obtained by the various lists competing for delegates' votes.[4] The only significant change has been the enfranchisement of regional party leaders as members of the selectorate within the Federal Political Committee who select the party leader. This change has its origins in internal strife too. It was introduced by Llamazares in the 2004 party conference when his list received 49.5 per cent of the delegates' votes but opposition factions' lists had two more votes than him in the Federal Political Committee. As the majority of the regional party leaders supported Llamazares, his re-election was thus assured (Ştefuriuc & Verge 2008, p. 164).

In 2008, five groups put up candidates lists. The one that best represented the PCE's most critical faction obtained 43 per cent of the delegates' votes, and the one that supported the former party leader 27 per cent. As no list obtained the majority of votes (over 50 per cent) of the elected members of the Federal Political Committee, the conference finished with no party leader elected. It took a month to reach a decision and it was finally the former opposition faction led by the PCE which managed to see its candidate, Cayo Lara, come out on top (Verge 2010, pp. 100–103).

Policy-making. From the early 1990s, the 'collective elaboration' of electoral manifestos, including the direct input of members and social movements, became one of the most significant party principles. IU began to create a new party structure of working groups (called *áreas*) responsible for the direct participation of individual members and non-members in policy-making. Working groups were linked to the different policy-making domains (economy, women, youth, environment, urban planning, etc.) and any member could be involved in any of them (in fact, the party urged members to be actively involved). The working groups were to maintain close links with social movements, which would be invited to participate.

The working groups, created at every territorial level of organisation, were accorded their own structures. Their relevance for the party was recognised by incorporating the coordinators of the working groups in IU's (local, regional and national) executive committees. The proposals drafted by the working groups, ideally a result of members' and social movements' involvement, were to be the basic inputs for electoral manifestos—to be eventually approved by the respective executive committee and by a programmatic party conference. IU public representatives, either in government or in opposition, were to be involved in the working groups related to their activity as well. In their work, IU parliamentary groups and even (local) governments as well as IU leadership bodies were to reflect and promote the policy proposals elaborated by the working groups.

However, analysis of the real functioning of party channels for the direct involvement of members in policy-making reveals several shortcomings. First, their creation was very slow and many of them still remain underdeveloped. By 1997 these working groups had not been created as yet in some regional branches, while in others they were not consolidated. Although this situation was corrected and working groups have now been developed throughout the organisation, their expansion to the local level, where citizen participation is more feasible, has been far from successful. Second, despite the working groups being designed as participatory bodies the number of members taking part in them has remained low. Similarly, participation of non-members and social movements in the working groups is rare. Their involvement seems to be reduced to particular occasions such as pre-electoral months or strong periods of mobilisation. As a consequence, those working groups which function regularly often resemble more a group of specialists, consultants or advisers than the participatory device they were intended to be. Third, the relationship of the working groups with IU leaders and public representatives has not been easy and has instead been uneven and unpredictable. Although in some instances collaboration and the policy proposals of the working group have prevailed, in other cases working groups have operated in disconnection from IU's public representatives, or, at most, the working groups (or some of their members) have acted as mere advisers to a particular public official (far away from their original grassroots democracy purpose).

Last, their relationship with IU leaders has been troublesome. One contentious issue was the creation by the IU leadership from the beginning of the 1990s—at the different territorial levels—of sectoral secretariats in charge of policy domains that overlap with the working groups (i.e. secretariats of economy, welfare, etc.). To a certain extent this has shown the incapacity of the working groups to play their original policy-making role. It has also been the result of the perceived need for the leadership to rely on a more agile and effective structure. Yet it also reflects the mistrust of the different party leaderships towards the working groups, as, in the context of a divided party, the latter have often become a battleground for factional disputes. After almost twenty years since the creation of this model of working groups for policy-making, it is still a contentious issue. During 2008 and 2009, when IU debated its possible 're-foundation' after the crushing electoral defeat of the 2008 election, the underdevelopment and paralysis of the working groups was once again discussed. Leaving aside the description of the working groups, this examination of policy-making procedures and of the role of members would be incomplete without mentioning that in the drafting of electoral manifestos a key role is played by party (senior) officials and MPs in the conventional way common to many parties. And, as in other organisations, party conferences are officially the main decision-making body.

Even if since 1994 the party conference mandate has been enlarged from two to three years, thus potentially reducing members' capacity to provide inputs, their influence did actually slightly increase with the acquisition of new rights. In 1997 IU granted members the right to make proposals to national organs and the right to be asked their opinion through a public consultation process on questions of 'special interest' for the party. In 2004 the right to call referendums, originally in the hands of the party's national bodies, was extended to regional executive committees and also to members' initiatives gathering the support of 30 per cent of the party membership. Yet, in practice, these new rights and procedures have had a limited impact on the decision-making process. A membership ballot was planned for September 2004 to decide the party position on the European Constitution Treaty, which the national government would submit to citizens' will in February 2005. In the end the party referendum was not scheduled, as it overlapped with an extraordinary party conference convoked after the disastrous electoral results obtained by IU in the 2004 general election. Instead, during this conference, party delegates ratified the party leadership's position which advocated a negative vote (Verge 2012b).

Although no membership ballots of this kind have ever been held at the national party level, two binding referendums were called by the regional organisation of Extremadura and by the provincial organisation of Alava to decide on IU's political strategy after the 2011 local and regional elections. In the case of Extremadura, the referendum brought about public conflict between the regional organisation and the national leadership as the results of the membership ballot contravened the latter's instruction to support the investiture of the PSOE candidate.[5] The event illustrates the vague statutory definition of these procedures, their lack of institutionalisation as well as the confusion regarding the distribution of powers between national bodies and regional party branches. It should be noted, though, that the national party leadership finally accepted the decision of the rank and file. Despite the controversial experience of this referendum, in 2012 two more regional branches, with the support of the national leadership, called the membership to cast a ballot on the eventual integration of IU in a coalition cabinet with the PSOE. Turnout was very high in Andalusia, reaching about 80 per cent of members, and more modest in Asturias, where just a third of the members cast a vote. Whereas in Asturias IU members rejected the option to join the regional government coalition as suggested by the regional and national leaderships and opted instead to support a PSOE cabinet from the opposition benches, in Andalusia the rank and file aligned with the regional and national leaderships and voted hugely in favour of the incorporation of IU into the regional government.[6] The results of the referendum were binding for the party leadership in both regions. The party could then present these results to public opinion as an exercise of intra-party democracy, which is not common at all amongst the other Spanish parties.

Environmental Linkage

Embedded in the political dimension of the new organisational project launched by the PCE was the goal of opening the traditional left towards a more intense relationship with civil society. Facing an acute electoral decline and having adopted participatory democratic ideals, how did the Spanish radical left redesign its environmental linkage strategy?

As mentioned above, IU's self-conception was that of a 'political and social movement' rather than a (traditional) political party. The creation of IU fostered change in the way the founding parties related to social groups. For example, from the 1960s, the PCE used its resources to organise Spanish civil society against the authoritarian regime (Encarnación 2003, p. 47). The organisations created by the PCE included the Movimiento Democrático de Mujeres (Democratic Movement of Women), pioneering the contemporary Spanish feminist movement, and the Movimiento Popular y Ciudadano (Popular and Citizen's Movement), a grassroots neighbourhood movement. But most important, the PCE also employed the nascent labour movement organised around the Comisiones Obreras (Workers' Commissions, CCOO), controlled by the party, as its key instrument in the fight against the dictatorship, penetrating the Francoist-sponsored unions and leading workers' mobilisation. The links between the PCE and CCOO materialised in the overlapping composition of their leaderships and rank and file and the presence of union leaders among public representatives, which allowed the party to have an important influence in the formulation of union policies (Fishman 1990, pp. 164–167).

In the 1980s, the PCE believed social presence was decisive for the implementation of Eurocommunism as well as to recover electoral support and stop membership losses.[7] Party cadres and activists were urged to foster social mobilisation as well as to spread the party message within social movements. In addition, the party sponsored the creation of various social organisations and exerted influence over others in the areas of feminism, environmentalism, pacifism and human rights through overlapping memberships and the presence of party members in leadership positions (Verge 2012a, p. 51). However, the proportion of communist members among the CCOO rank and file gradually decreased and leadership overlaps dramatically diminished—until their near disappearance as the PCE suffered internal divisions and splits and experienced a deep electoral decline and the CCOO chose to increase its autonomy from political parties. The weakening of communist influence on other social organisations was even more acute.

Conversely, IU has not sponsored the creation of collateral social organisations.[8] Still, close ties with social movements are considered of paramount importance to foster social mobilisation. IU was born in 1986 after the success obtained by the Civic Platform for Spain's exit from the North Atlantic Treaty Organisation (NATO), in which the PCE participated with other left-wing social and political groupings.[9] Policy innovation and the pursuit of a new type of linkage were interconnected strategies to counteract the electoral decline of the party. The adoption in the 1980s of new political issues was accompanied by a discourse that highlighted the relevance of linkage with civil society organisations and of social mobilisation. However, the growth of the political autonomy of civil society organisations and the weakening of the PCE organisations obliged IU to approach civil society in a very different manner to that of the PCE in the 1970s.

Linkage with civil society materialised through various mechanisms. First, the participation of social groups in the design of party manifestos was to be channelled through the working groups or *áreas*, as we have already discussed, in which not only would inputs be provided but also joint social mobilisation would be planned. Second, the party adopted a collaborative strategy as it perceived increased autonomy demands from civil society. This is illustrated by CCOO's rejection of the PCE's and IU's interference on the definition of its policies (Ramiro 2004b, p. 22).[10] Throughout the 1990s, IU participated in several social platforms such as the 'Civic Platform for Social Rights' (1995–98), articulated against the labour reform approved by the socialist government, and was also an active member of the 'Citizens Network for the Abolition of (third world) External Debt', and the 'Platform for the 0.7' (1994), which urged national governments to devote 0.7 per cent of their countries' gross domestic product (GDP) to third world aid. In 1994 IU also launched the 'Taskforce for a Green and Alternative Left' composed of party members and social activists. It aimed at mirroring the anti-NATO social mobilisations of the 1980s, the target being on this occasion the 1994 European elections, though success was rather limited (Verge 2007, p. 280). Party candidatures were even offered to social activists (Pastor 2004, p. 35), an opening that the PCE had also attempted in the 1980s. Once again, the IU leadership aimed at translating social mobilisation into electoral mobilisation, which would eventually lead to IU surpassing the PSOE and establishing itself as the main left-wing party. The political recruitment of social activists was also thought to offer prestige and credibility to the party's electoral tickets. Yet the party's electoral expectations were clearly overestimated, as Table 1 shows.

From 1996 onwards, IU joined several social platforms against the conservative government and launched common proposals with social groups. It joined the Social Forum and the platform against the Iraq War. New party secretariats were established from the late 1990s, partially with a view to forging ties with social organisations (Social Movements, Ecology, International Solidarity, Human Rights, and Globalisation and Youth). Finally, as in many other parties, IU has traditionally invited social representatives to party conferences.

Although IU has tried to foster the social activism of its members as a means of picking up on social demands and of keeping left-wing voters mobilised—indeed many IU members are activists in a broad array of social groups—the party does not keep any record of their participation, so the potential feedback is lost. Besides not having created social organisations of its own, IU has also lost influence over those groups the PCE had long controlled through overlapping memberships, partly due to decreasing membership levels and partly due to increasing autonomy demands from civil society organisations. In addition, party factionalism has often led to a fragmented social presence, with no clear political direction or strategy, which has often impeded IU in its efforts to bridge social demands. For example, internal disputes were often brought into the global justice movement, with one of the competing factions trying to instrumentalise the support of this movement in its favour (Verge 2010, p. 97).

With the exception of the 1980s, in the context of the anti-NATO social mobilisations and the general strikes against the PSOE government, IU has been unable to capitalise on discontented voters' support in any significant way. Several social platforms were created against the right-wing Partido Popular (Popular Party, PP) government (1996–2004, especially since 2000 onwards) on issues like secondary education and university reform, labour reform and the Iraq War. Although these social platforms provided for various meeting points of the party with civil society, in the 2004 and 2008 national legislative elections a significant proportion of former IU voters opted for the PSOE (Font & Ramiro 2011). Therefore, episodes of high social mobilisation and IU's efforts to connect the party with social movements did not result in relevant electoral gains. This outcome can be explained by the general patterns of Spaniards' electoral behaviour and wider factors affecting voters' calculations, such as strategic voting, voters' ideology and parties' policies (Font & Ramiro 2011), rather than by the specific strategies of IU towards social movements and the levels of social mobilisation, which are much less influential determinants of electoral fortunes.

Another opportunity to forge links was the referendum for the European Constitution, when IU sided with the camp of 'No' supporters, basically consisting of minor left-wing and some nationalist parties along with the global justice movement and other social organisations. The 'No' position, given Spaniards' embedded pro-European political culture, was not based on Euroscepticism but on claims that the European Constitutional Treaty was inadequate to protect social and workers' rights and that it did not do enough to address the European Union's democratic deficit, among other issues (Benedetto & Quaglia 2007, p. 493; Verge 2012b, p. 83). Eventually, the number of positive votes was vast, 76.7 per cent, and about a third of IU voters also supported the European Constitution against the party's official position (European Commission 2005, p. 16).

After the 2008 disastrous electoral results, the party admitted that change was urgently needed and all factions unanimously agreed to the 're-foundation' of IU. One of the secretariats of the national executive board was entrusted with organising a constituent assembly by mid-2010 and establishing working groups at the different territorial levels of the party, aimed at discussing how to re-found the party and to strengthen its political-and-social-movement nature. Social groups opposing neo-liberalism were also invited to put forward their contributions for the renewed project. Particularly, IU targeted feminist, environmental, pacifist, human rights, and lesbian, gay, bisexual and transgender organisations, unions, neighbourhood and students associations, as well as social groups that advocate an alternative economy and those in favour of the abolition of the monarchy (IU 2009). Actually, according to party sources, 40 per cent of the 1,000 delegates at the 're-foundation assembly' held in June 2010 were not party members and about 60 social organisations were invited to participate.[11]

Although it is too soon to assess the impact of the re-foundation process, three years after the goal was established no significant results have been produced and many regional party branches are completely disconnected from it. Some party factions have repeatedly denounced the shortcomings of its implementation and its incapacity to appeal to social groups and to other parties of the left. In fact, IU has suffered new splits in several regions in recent years (Valencia, Balearic Islands and the Basque Country), and the splinter groups have not taken part in the re-foundation process, so we may wonder how inclusive this process has been. In any case, the process has been insufficient to deter internal strife.

Finally, the social mobilisations that developed on the eve of the May 2011 local and regional elections were mainly led by politically disaffected youngsters angry at massive unemployment and austerity measures who established protest camps and open-air sit-ins in the main cities. While these were among the most relevant social and political mobilisations in recent years, IU and other left-wing parties were absent in their preparation and development. Although IU made some electoral gains in the 2011 local and regional elections and even managed to obtain seats in a couple of regional parliaments where it had been an extra-parliamentary force since 2003, the results do not point to a very significant improvement. Regarding local elections, in those cities where the movement was stronger the main consequence was that the number of invalid and blank votes increased, even if IU also slightly improved its results (Jiménez 2011).

Yet it is too soon to assess whether the party might be able to connect with this spontaneous and organisationally decentralised movement which has progressively adopted some of the traditional radical left programmatic issues. On the one hand, even if IU was the most voted-for party among the participants of the Indignados (Outraged movement) (Martín 2012), the latter claim to be a movement independent of any political party. Finally, it also remains to be seen how this movement may evolve and whether it can last given its weak to non-existent organisational structures. In any case, many of the most recent waves of anti-austerity mobilisations that developed in late 2011 and during 2012 are mainly led by more traditional actors (unions) that are less reluctant to cooperate with parties. Therefore, IU already enjoys a certain visibility in these mobilisations, as the issues at stake—such as protests against labour reform or against the cuts in the provision of public social services—are certainly some of the most relevant issues in IU's discourse, and this provides a good opportunity for IU to strengthen its environmental linkages.

Conclusion

The PCE responded to its electoral and organisational crisis by creating a new organisation in 1986, IU, which has explicitly and repeatedly tried to improve and reinforce its participatory and environmental linkages. This strategy should be placed in the context of the electoral decline of Western communist parties and the decisions adopted by some of them in order to survive in an increasingly hostile external electoral and organisational environment and while facing acute internal strife. In several cases these parties have moved towards more open organisations, ideologically closer to new politics issues, with more empowered members, and with a clear will to strengthen ties with social organisations.

This article has analysed the formal definition and practical implementation of the IU strategies aimed at strengthening the linkage processes. Given the centrality of these strategies in the party's political project and identity, the shortcomings identified are certainly notable. Regarding participatory linkage, IU tried to give form to a new type of organisation in which citizens and grassroots members would play a relevant role in decision-making. However, the actions implemented to empower members have failed not only to attract new members but also to alter the internal distribution of power, as we have discussed. The limited ambition of the changes and the constraints facing their implementation clearly stand out. In some key aspects the role of members has grown very modestly. The definition of primaries is still vague and confusing, the leadership is not obliged to promote them and there is no clear regulation of their implementation. The traditional procedure for selecting leaders by the party conference and the Federal Political Committee remains intact. Certainly, given their actual implementation, some of the actions designed to reinforce participatory linkage can hardly be considered appealing incentives to boost party membership. Leaders and factions have strategically promoted some procedures for members' participation, as shown in the institutional underdevelopment of primaries, their scarce and erratic use and their frequent employment as an additional device in party infighting. Only the recently introduced membership ballots to decide on the party's governing strategy in the regions where the party was a pivotal actor, which is an exceptional practice in the Spanish context, shows a significant—although still partial—empowerment of party members.

Evaluation of the strategies aimed at reinforcing environmental linkage also points to difficulty in implementation. Although IU leaders have constantly insisted on the relevance of maintaining close ties with social organisations, this has proved an elusive goal with dubious results. While the PCE sponsored a number of social organisations from the 1960s until the 1980s, IU adopted an alternative approach promoting instead more informal and less exclusive ties with social groups. The difference between the two parties is largely due to their different organisational models as well as the fact that civil society in Western countries has become very reluctant to maintain close links with parties and, consequently, parties struggle to perform their environmental linkage function (Ramiro & Morales 2010). Besides, IU's contribution to social mobilisation in Spain has been undecisive—if not irrelevant—and has often been a divisive element associated with infighting.

Finally, what does the IU experiment, being one of the oldest case studies included in this special issue, show us regarding the extent to which environmental linkage can work, nowadays, at least for the radical left party family? Overall, the party strategies aimed at reinforcing linkage have not sufficed to guarantee the stabilisation of IU's electoral fortunes at levels such that its survival can be ensured or membership losses deterred. While the impulse and design of strategies rely to a large extent on the party's own decisions, their results crucially depend on environmental factors in which parties can hardly intervene (such as the strategies of their main competitors or the long-term evolution of public opinion). However, the very same strategies of IU (and of the PCE, as the key actor within the IU) have suffered from important flaws since the very beginning, and these have hindered their success. The implementation of participatory linkage strategies has been very modest in some aspects and clearly defective in others, partly due to their instrumental (ab)use in factional disputes, and they have failed to produce any significant change in the internal balance of power or to stimulate membership growth. Likewise, the strategies towards civil society have tended to overstate the party's organisational resources and its capacity to influence social movements, and have disregarded the strong preference for autonomy from political parties that civil society organisations show. In this vein, although the social mobilisations that the economic crisis has brought about in Southern Europe offer an opportunity to reconnect with society, radical left parties must avoid giving the impression that relationships with social groups are established for mere strategic electoral reasons.

Acknowledgements

The authors would like to thank the editors of this special issue as well as the anonymous reviewers for their useful comments on a previous draft of this article.

Notes

[1] Besides the PCE, there are currently only some very small parties, such as Izquierda Abierta (Open Left), created in 2012 around the IU MP and former leader Gaspar Llamazares, and the Colectivo de Unidad de los Trabajadores–Bloque Andaluz de Izquierdas (Workers' Unity Collective–Andalusian Left Block), an Andalusian extreme left party.

[2] Regional branches are in charge of the selection of candidates for their electoral districts, the Federal Executive Committee being responsible for the final approval of the candidate tickets.

[3] See 'IU de Jaén elige a su candidato con primarias abiertas a simpatizantes', *El País*, 3 June 2006; 'IU Valladolid, pionera en abrir sus listas a los ciudadanos', *El Mundo*, 19 February 2010.

[4] The rest of the members of the Federal Political Committee are nominated by the party's regional branches. Regional party leaders also sit on this board. The total composition of the Federal Political Committee is limited to a maximum number of 180 members by the party statutes.

[5] See 'IU Extremadura desafía a Cayo Lara', *Público*, 3 June 2011.

[6] On the Andalusian referendum, see 'El 84,9% de la militancia de IU aprueba un Gobierno de coalición con el PSOE', *El País*, 25 April 2012. On the Asturian referendum, see 'La militancia de IU rechaza por 16 votos gobernar con el PSOE en Asturias', *El Mundo*, 25 May 2012.

[7] 'Eurocommunism' is the term commonly used to refer to a strategy promoted by some Western Communist parties (originally the French, the Italian and the Spanish ones) during the 1970s and the 1980s, consisting in a dealignment from the policies of the Soviet Union and in the acceptance of democratic political institutions and procedures to gain power. Aimed at adapting the communist credo to the realities of Western societies, it entailed, in several regards, a sort of 'social-democratisation' of their ideology.

[8] Though we might think that political and social changes render this strategy impossible, the PSOE still used it during the 1990s and the PP has not abandoned it yet (Verge 2012b).

[9] The PSOE national government had initially defended withdrawal from NATO in 1981 but once in office it supported Spain's permanent place in this military alliance. The referendum (March 1986) yielded a minimal victory for remaining in NATO but seven million Spaniards cast a no vote. These were precisely the voters IU targeted.

[10] The growing ideological gap between CCOO and the PCE and IU, a phenomenon common to other West European parties and unions, included episodes of harsh confrontation during the 1990s. Subsequent strategies aimed at rebuilding the union–party relationship have not been able to halt a dynamic of the separation of CCOO from any link with any party, this being rooted in deep political and social changes. Their relationship has evolved from one of close coordination and overlapping leadership to one of mere policy coincidence—and not even that on all the relevant social and economic issues—in tune with the general trend in party–union relationships in Western Europe (Poguntke 2002).

[11] See 'IU busca construir un movimiento de personas y fuerzas de izquierdas para responder a los ataques que sufre la mayoría social y los trabajadores', available online at: http://www.izquierda-unida.es/node/7590 (accessed 20 July 2011).

References

Allern, E. H. (2010) *Political Parties and Interest Groups in Norway*, ECPR Press, Colchester.

Allern, E. H. & Bale, T. (2012) 'Political parties and interest groups: disentangling complex relationships', *Party Politics*, vol. 18, no. 1, pp. 7–25.

Bell, D. S. (ed.) (1993) *Western European Communists and the Collapse of Communism*, Berg, Oxford.

Benedetto, G. & Quaglia, L. (2007) 'The comparative politics of communist Euroscepticism in France, Spain and Italy', *Party Politics*, vol. 13, no. 4, pp. 479–500.

Bosco, A. (2000) *Comunisti. Trasformazioni di partito in Italia, Spagna e Portogallo*, Il Mulino, Bologna.

Botella, J. & Ramiro, L. (eds) (2003) *The Crisis of Communism and Party Change: The Evolution of Western European Communist and Post-Communist Parties*, Institut de Ciències Polítiques i Socials, Barcelona.

Bull, M. & Heywood, P. (eds) (1994) *West European Communist Parties after the Revolutions of 1989*, St Martin Press, New York.

Dalton, R. J. & Wattenberg, M. P. (eds) (2000) *Parties without Partisans: Political Change in Advanced Industrial Democracies*, Oxford University Press, Oxford.

Encarnación, O. G. (2003) *The Myth of Civil Society. Social Capital and Democratic Consolidation in Spain and Brazil*, Palgrave, New York.

European Commission. (2005) 'The European Constitution: post-referendum survey in Spain', Flash Eurobarometer 168, available online at: http://ec.europa.eu/public_opinion/flash/fl_168_en.pdf (accessed 26 September 2012)

Fishman, R. M. (1990) *Working-Class Organization and the Return to Democracy in Spain*, Cornell University Press, Ithaca, NY.

Font, J. & Ramiro, L. (2011) 'La concentración del voto de izquierdas: ¿cambio de preferencias o voto útil?', in *Elecciones Generales 2008*, eds J. R. Montero & I. Lago, Centro de Investigaciones Sociológicas, Madrid, pp. 207–233.

IU (2009) 'Guía participativa para la refundación de la izquierda', available online at: http://izquierda-unida.es/sites/default/files/doc/ GUÍA%20PARTICIPATIVA%20PARA%20LA%20REFUNDACIÓN%20DE%20LA%20IZQUIERDA.pdf> (accessed 15 May 2010)

Jiménez, M. (2011) 'Especial 15M. ¿Influyó el 15M en las elecciones municipales?', *Zoom Político*, no. 4, pp. 18–28.

Katz, R. S. & Mair, P. (1995) 'Changing models of party organization and party democracy: the emergence of the cartel party', *Party Politics*, vol. 1, no. 1, pp. 5–28.

Kitschelt, H. (1994) *The Transformation of European Social Democracy*, Cambridge University Press, Cambridge.

Lawson, K. (1980) *Political Parties and Linkage: A Comparative Perspective*, Yale University Press, New Haven.

Martín, I. (2012) 'Political disaffection revisited: the *Indignant* movement in Spain, or a different way of doing politics', paper presented at the conference 'Voting and Protesting in Europe since 2008', Georgetown University, Washington, 17–18 April 2012.

Méndez, M., Morales, L. & Ramiro, L. (2004) 'Los afiliados y su papel en los partidos políticos españoles', *Zona Abierta*, no. 108–109, pp. 153–207.

Merkl, P. H. (2005) 'Linkage, or what else? The place of linkage theory in the study of political parties', in *Political Parties and Political Systems: The Concept of Linkage Revisited*, eds A. Römmele, D. M. Farrell & P. Ignazi, Praeger, Westport, CT, pp. 3–16.

Paniagua, J. L. & Ramiro, L. (2003) *Voz, conflicto y salida. Un estudio sobre faccionalismo: Nueva Izquierda, 1992–2001*, Editorial Complutense, Madrid.

Pastor, J. (2004) 'Evolución, crisis y mutaciones de la izquierda transformadora y alternativa', *Mientras Tanto*, no. 91–92, pp. 29–44.

Poguntke, T. (2002) 'Party organisational linkage: parties without firm social roots?', in *Political Parties in the New Europe: Political and Analytical Challenges*, eds K. R. Luther & F. Müller-Rommel, Oxford University Press, Oxford, pp. 43–62.

Ramiro, L. (2000) 'Entre coalición y partido: la evolución del modelo organizativo de Izquierda Unida', *Revista Española de Ciencia Política*, vol. 1, no. 2, pp. 237–268.

Ramiro, L. (2004a) *Cambio y adaptación en la izquierda. La evolución del Partido Comunista de España y de Izquierda Unida (1986–2000)*, Centro de Investigaciones Sociológicas, Madrid.

Ramiro, L. (2004b) 'Electoral competition, organizational constraints and party change: The Communist Party of Spain (PCE) and United Left (IU), 1986–2000', *Journal of Communist and Transition Politics*, vol. 20, no. 2, pp. 1–29.

Ramiro, L. & Morales, L. (2010) 'Spanish parties and democracy: weak party–society linkage and intense party–state symbiosis', in *Political Parties and Democracy*, ed. K. Lawson, Praeger/Greenwood, Westport, CT, pp. 71–96.

Scarrow, S. E., Webb, P. & Farrell, D. M. (2000) 'From social integration to electoral contestation: the changing distribution of power within political parties', in *Parties without Partisans. Political Change in Advanced Industrial Democracies*, eds R. J. Dalton & M. Wattenberg, Oxford University Press, Oxford, pp. 129–154.

Schwartz, M. A. (2005) 'Linkage processes in party networks', in *Political Parties and Political Systems: The Concept of Linkage Revisited*, eds A. Römmele, D. M. Farrell & P. Ignazi, Praeger, Westport, CT, pp. 37–60.

Ştefuriuc, I. & Verge, T. (2008) 'Small and divided parties in multi-level settings: opportunities for government participation, the case of Izquierda Unida in Spain', *South European Society and Politics*, vol. 13, no. 2, pp. 155–173.

Thomas, C. S. (ed.) (2001) *Political Parties and Interest Groups: Shaping Democratic Governance*, Lynne Rienner, Boulder.

Verge, T. (2007) *Partidos y representación política: Las dimensiones del cambio en los partidos políticos españoles, 1976–2006*, Centro de Investigaciones Sociológicas, Madrid.

Verge, T. (2010) 'The Spanish United Left – the belated and troublesome transition from policy-seeking to office-seeking', in *Left Parties in National Governments*, eds J. Olsen, M. Koss & D. Hough, Palgrave, Basingstoke, pp. 87–104.

Verge, T. (2012a) 'Party strategies towards civil society in new democracies: the Spanish case', *Party Politics*, vol. 18, no. 1, pp. 45–60.

Verge, T. (2012b) 'Left parties and the European Constitution in Spain: building and contesting Europe from a federalist perspective', in *The Left and the European Constitution: From Laeken to Lisbon*, eds K. Roder & M. Holmes, Manchester University Press, Manchester, pp. 77–94.

Verge, T. & Gómez, R. (2012) 'Factionalism in multi-level contexts: when party organisation becomes a device', *Party Politics*, vol. 18, no. 5, pp. 667–685.

Waller, M. & Fennema, M. (eds) (1988) *Communist Parties in Western Europe. Decline or Adaptation*, Basil Blackwell, Oxford.

Yishai, Y. (2001) 'Bringing society back in. Post-cartel parties in Israel', *Party Politics*, vol. 7, no. 6, pp. 667–687.

Luis Ramiro (PhD European University Institute, Florence) is Associate Professor of Political Science at the University of Murcia, Spain. His research focuses on political behaviour, organisations and parties and he has published extensively on these topics in relation to the Spanish case. Some of his most recent publications have appeared in journals such as *Mobilization* and *Party Politics*.

Tània Verge is a Lecturer in the Department of Political and Social Sciences at the Universitat Pompeu Fabra (Barcelona). Her research interests concentrate on party politics and gender and politics. She is the author of several national and international publications that focus on party organisation and on women's presence in public institutions and political parties.

Renewal and Tradition: Comparing Italian Radical Left Parties through their Middle-Level Elites

Paola Bordandini

The article analyses the current Italian radical left parties—Federation of the Left and Left Ecology and Freedom—to understand how they are similar, how they differ and why. The analysis is based on data from 644 responses of party delegates gathered in 2010 at the first national conventions of the two parties. The paper (i) reconstructs the complex origin of the two parties; (ii) compares their organisational structures; (iii) analyses their ability to involve their members in the party decision-making process; and (iv) examines the relationships between the two parties and organisations of civil society.

After the end of the Cold War, the dissolution of the Partito Comunista Italiano (Italian Communist Party, PCI) and the transformations of the Italian political system as a whole, the Italian radical left underwent profound changes at the organisational, ideological and strategic levels (Bosco 2001; March 2011). Over the past 15 years and amid splits and new combinations, even the most 'orthodox' successors of the old PCI changed in part their ideological reference points, broadened their political agendas, promoted new organisational tools and assumed direct governmental responsibilities in 1998 and 2006.

The literature on party change points out how Western parties have gradually lost their ties to civil society (Katz & Mair 1995). However, one notes, especially in the parties of the European radical left, a stated commitment to implement strategies capable of reversing this trend (Bosco 2000; Botella & Ramiro 2003).

This article aims to analyse the extent to which the two current parties of the Italian radical left—the Federazione della Sinistra (Federation of the Left, FDS) and Sinistra Ecologia e Libertà (Left Ecology and Freedom, SEL)—are similar and how they differ in relation to the ties they shape with their members, with their voters and, more generally, with civil society. The analysis makes reference to the concept of party linkage (Lawson 1980; Römmele, Farrell & Ignazi 2005), using an examination of the parties' statutes and of survey data regarding the attitudes of the middle-level party elites of the two parties as an empirical foundation. The perspective of party linkage is pursued with reference to both participatory and environmental linkages. In other words, I will analyse how SEL and FDS shape their relationships with party members and with organised civil society and, more generally, how they perceive their representational function.

The use of an empirical analysis focused on statutory norms, and on the opinions and attitudes of the middle-level elites, offers more than one advantage. Both SEL and FDS were established only recently; therefore, their electoral and membership data cannot provide suitably significant information on the forms of linkage that the parties are pursuing. The middle-level elites, on the other hand, represent the most stable stratum of party organisation and their members usually maintain significant ties with civil society. Therefore, an examination of the intermediate elites allows one to advance an empirically founded opinion on the linkages that a party builds with civil society and with social groups.

The work is structured as follows. In the first section, I describe the empirical data on which the article is based. In the second, I trace a brief historical profile of the two parties, in order to identify their direct and indirect links to the old PCI. The third section deals with participatory linkage and intra-party democracy. By examining the statutes and founding documents of the two parties I will present their main organisational features and the opinions and attitudes of the respondents with regard to their party. The fourth section—dedicated to environmental linkage—will highlight the two parties' links to social movements and organised civil society. The concluding section will trace a comparative profile of the two parties based not only on their organisational structure and on the manner in which they exercise their participatory and environmental linkages, but also on their prospects for the future.

The Empirical Foundation: A Comparison of Party Delegates

National party delegates represent a central segment of the organisational framework of political parties; the party transformations of the last decades may have diminished somewhat the importance of this segment and modified its characteristics, but it remains, nevertheless, a significant unit of analysis for the parties under consideration. This is particularly the case if one wants to examine more closely the linkage between parties and civil society. National party delegates are, in fact, not merely members, but also activists with a long history of political militancy and, in many cases, with experience in appointed or elected positions in politics and in local and regional associations. In other words, they represent nodal elements of the civic and party communities, capable of shedding light on the relationships between parties and society and between local party and central organisation. Party delegates can also be considered privileged witnesses who have experienced from within the transformations of the parties. Their opinions, values and attitudes are, therefore, more elaborate and more stable than those of members as a whole. In many cases, moreover, they represent a bridge between older and newer party formations. For these reasons, national party delegates are a critical object of observation for studying parties and their different linkages with civil society (Bordandini & Di Virgilio 2007; Bordandini, Di Virgilio & Mulè 2011).

The empirical foundation of this paper is based on 644 questionnaire responses gathered during the first national convention of SEL (Florence, 22–24 October 2010) and the first national convention of the FDS (Rome, 20–21 November 2010).[1] These samples display robust coverage—the 259 respondents of FDS represent 43 per cent of the total population of delegates to the first convention, while the 385 respondents of SEL represent 44 per cent of the total, confidence intervals ranging between ± 3.7 per cent for SEL and ± 4.6 per cent for FDS (with a confidence level of 95 per cent).[2] Moreover, these are easily comparable samples. Their distributions with respect to key socio-demographic characteristics (gender, age, education, area of residence, profession) are actually rather balanced, and this fact, besides highlighting the social homogeneity of the middle-level elite of the two parties, makes it easier to analyse the data being presented, since it is possible to rely on the parameterisation at the source of these structural variables.

The differences between the two samples are marginal and involve mainly the delegates' distributions with respect to gender (the SEL sample contains 35 per cent of female delegates, compared with 26 per cent for the FDS sample) and educational level (48 per cent of FDS delegates hold a university degree, compared with 57 per cent of SEL delegates, but only just under six per cent of both parties' delegates ended their studies after the obligatory educational cycle). The average age, though, is essentially the same (46 for FDS and 45 for SEL), as is the median one (47 for both parties). Of limited significance are the differences in the area of residence and in the professional profile of the two groups of delegates. One notable aspect, in terms of differences between the two samples, is the higher percentage of party (or union) officials within FDS (12 per cent) compared with SEL (five per cent). Also noteworthy is the coincidence in both samples of the percentage of delegates who work in the public sector (approximately 40 per cent), of those who work in white-collar jobs (24 per cent) and of those who work in blue-collar jobs (slightly above four per cent).

FDS and SEL: Their Birth Certificates

Though the two contemporary parties of the Italian radical left share a common DNA, this does not authorise us to consider them simply as children, cousins or grandchildren of the old PCI. The path to their creation is so full of splits and fusions that the complexity of their family relationships is akin to that of the Buendía family in *One Hundred Years of Solitude* by Gabriel García Márquez. Within each of the two parties, in fact, one finds components whose respective positions with regard to policy priorities, oppositional strategy, inter-party competition and alliances went from political harmony to bitter discord within the space of a few years.

Thus, it is not easy to reconstruct the history of the two parties in a few lines. It is necessary to begin in 1989, when the General Secretary of the PCI, Achille Occhetto, dissolved the party. Two parties arose from its ashes: the Partito Democratico della Sinistra (Party of the Democrats of the Left, PDS) and the Partito della Rifondazione Comunista (Communist Refoundation Party, PRC).[3] The PDS, as eldest child of the PCI, inherited a large part of the organisational structure of its parent, putting immediately into motion, however, both a process of ideological de-radicalisation and one of profound organisational metamorphosis. Such transformations were marked by the change of the party symbol in 1998—with the transition from the PDS to the Democratici di Sinistra (Democrats of the Left, DS) the communist symbols of sickle and hammer were removed—and in 2007 by the merger—together with the Margherita (Daisy, inheritor party of the left wing of the Italian Christian Democratic Party)—into the Partito Democratico (Democratic Party, PD). In this latter passage, the DS suffered the splitting away of the Sinistra Democratica (Democratic Left, SD).

The path followed by the PRC is no less convoluted. This party gathered several leaders and factions of the old PCI, and of small radical leftist political groupings outside the PCI, in the name of protecting a generic and differently conceived communist identity. The party leadership was diarchic right from the start. The President, Armando Cossutta, was the leader of the party wing that was the guardian of the ideological and organisational orthodoxy of the PCI; the Secretary, Sergio Garavini, personified the party's desire for renewal. Amid internal and external challenges, the PRC would constantly be characterised by the presence of factions. The party was divided not only with respect to which ideological-organisational orientation to promote, but also in regard to the possibility of entering the cabinet. Indeed, the issue of whether to support the centre-left government in office caused the two (parliamentary) splits that swept through the PRC in the 1990s. The first one in 1995 led to the establishment of the Movimento dei Comunisti Unitari (Movement of the Unitary Communists, MCU), which later merged into the DS; the second one in 1998 led to the creation of an outright new party, custodian of the memory of the PCI: the Partito dei Comunisti Italiani (Party of the Italian Communists, PDCI). In the following years, the PRC—pursuing the orientation of its leader, Fausto Bertinotti, who favoured strengthening links with social movements—began to emancipate itself from the old communist subcultural consensus.

In 2006, the success of Bertinotti's party was simultaneously electoral and political-institutional. It entered into the centre-left coalition led by Prodi (the Union), along with the PDCI and the Greens, and became a full member of the executive with one minister, Paolo Ferrero, and seven deputy ministers. The early elections of 2008, however, caught the entire Italian radical left off guard, forcing it to 'run alone' (since the newly born PD had decided to do the same).[4] This led to the creation of an electoral cartel that united all movements of the Italian left and radical left (Greens and former leftist DS included): the Sinistra Arcobaleno (Rainbow Left, SA) with Bertinotti as candidate for the premiership.[5] This operation was carried out badly, both in the selection of candidates and in the conduction of the campaign (Di Virgilio 2010), leading to a disastrous defeat: for the first time, the Parliament of the Italian Republic would not contain any representative of the organised radical left.

The defeat exacerbated the conflicts within the single parties, which convened furious conventions that produced break-ups, splits and new formations. As for the PRC, Bertinotti resigned from the party leadership and Nichi Vendola (his right hand) ran for the secretaryship of the party. At the national convention of 2008, Vendola led the majority wing, supported by over 43 per cent of the national delegates. The alliance of four minority factions, however, was able to block his election and impose the appointment of the orthodox Ferrero as secretary general. At this point, Vendola resigned from the PRC and founded the Movimento per la Sinistra (Movement for the Left, MpS). A similar break-up occurred within the PDCI with the departure of Unire la Sinistra (Unite the Left, UlS). At issue were two opposing strategic and organisational visions. One involved creating a new leftist political movement open to groups and movements to the left of the PD (as argued by Vendola and the political exiles from the PDCI) from the ashes of SA. The second one involved giving life to a new party founded principally on the unity of communists (as argued by Ferrero and the Secretary of the PDCI, Oliviero Diliberto). The diverging reactions to this issue led to the formation, in view of the European parliamentary elections of 2009, of two different groupings: Sinistra e Libertà (Left and Freedom, SL) and the Lista Comunista Anticapitalista (Anti-Capitalist Communist List), which can be considered the precursors, respectively, of SEL and FDS.

FDS was officially established as a federal political force on 5 December 2009. The Federation comprises four political entities: PRC, PDCI, Socialism 2000 (ex-DS) and the Association 'March 23 Labour-Solidarity' (the union component). Its leadership is collective. At the regional elections of 2010, FDS elected 17 regional councillors, coalescing with the centre-left led by the PD in 13 regions, with SEL in the Marche, and running independently in Lombardy and Campania. At the end of 2010, it had approximately 65,000 members.

SEL was established as a party on 20 December 2009 out of the merger of four organisations: SD (ex-DS), MpS (ex-PRC), UlS (ex-PDCI) and the Association of Ecologists (ex-Greens). Its undisputed leader was Nichi Vendola. At the regional elections of 2010, SEL elected 18 regional councillors and ran with its own lists in nine regions out of 13, coalescing in almost every case with the centre-left. Following the local elections of 2011 and 2012, SEL distinguished itself by winning, with the mayoral candidates Pisapia, Zedda and Doria, the municipalities of Milan, Cagliari and Genoa. In all these cases, SEL's candidates came out ahead, at the expense of PD representatives, in the 'coalition primaries' adopted to choose the mayoral candidates of the centre-left coalition.[6] At the end of 2010, SEL had over 45,600 members.

Both FDS and SEL are parties born through the aggregation of distinct political organisations, but, in terms of internal cohesion, there is a substantial difference between them. Whereas SEL can rely on the unifying power of an undisputed charismatic leader, FDS—as we shall see—must deal with the rigidity of a collegial leadership. On the other hand, FDS—since it contains two parties that have been on the political scene for over 10 (PDCI) and 20 (PRC) years—has a much broader party organisational structure than SEL.

These different strengths favour the predominance of different forms of linkage between party and society in the two parties. In SEL, the 'charismatic' party elite are more inclined to establish a direct linkage with voters, exploiting the media and the web. Conversely, the FDS party elite are more inclined to seek an indirect linkage with voters—an organisational linkage, as defined by Poguntke (2002)—mediated by the party membership organisation and by collateral organisations. After all, the very political project of FDS—along with its ties to communist tradition—discourages any kind of personalisation of politics. It privileges, instead, the party's programmatic offer, which emerges from a process of extensive negotiation within its ranks.

A Comparison of Leaderships and Statutes: Participatory Linkage

Participatory linkage concerns the ability of a party to involve its members in the party decision-making process (Lawson 1980). Therefore, it concerns intra-party democracy and the procedures employed for the selection of party leaders and party candidates, as well as the extent to which the party organisation allows members (and non-members) to be involved in the formulation of its programme (Heidar & Saglie 2003a; 2003b). In this section, I will examine how SEL and FDS exercise their participatory linkage, using the analysis of their statutes and the opinions of their middle-level elites as a starting point.

FDS is an association of parties based on collective leadership. Indeed, its statute is strongly oriented towards protecting the parity of associated components and towards keeping internal equilibria unchanged. By statute, the federated entities (PRC, PDCI, Socialism 2000 and the Association 'March 23 Labour-Solidarity')

> are part of the governing bodies and ... as a rule appoint equally and directly 25 per cent [of the members] of the political councils at all levels. The representatives of the federated entities are de jure members of the governing bodies at equivalent levels. As a rule, no federated organisation can express an absolute majority of the components in the political councils. (FDS 2010, Article 4)

At the central level, the structure comprises a political council (the deliberative party body with 117 members elected by the national convention), a national coordinating body (the executive party body elected by the political council) and a spokesperson (also elected by the political council). The spokesperson's task is to express 'the political line of FDS as indicated by the political council' (FDS 2010, Article 14). The national spokespersons are changed approximately every six months. The decision-making procedures are also geared towards safeguarding the rights of the various components of FDS. Any decision

> regarding any act of FDS, at any organisational level, requires (as a rule) a qualified majority of three-quarters of those voting ... if it is not possible for the body to take a decision on a specific issue, the same act can be submitted to the members by means of a referendum. (FDS 2010, Article 4)

The party organisation is structured in an orthodox manner, with federations at provincial and regional levels, and with 'houses of the left' and workers' circles (aggregated at a company or inter-company level) at local levels. The local organisations are open to supporters (be they single individual, associations or movements), although the right to vote is substantially restricted to members in the case of 'houses of the left'.

The primacy of party officials and the financial obligations of party representatives are set in traditional term:

> All public administrators and all those elected to institutions ... of FDS are accountable to the respective governing bodies of FDS for their mandate and, at the moment of acceptance of the candidacy ... undertake to pay the quota of any compensation for office and of any remuneration received due to the mandate itself, as established by an apposite Regulation ... The failure to comply with the above mentioned subscription duty is punished with expulsion from FDS. (FDS 2010, Article 20)

However, one cannot speak of FDS as a party that is hierarchical and centralised in its choice of candidates:

> All decisions related to electoral issues require the favourable vote of three-quarters of those voting [belonging to the political council], provided the legal number is met. The approval of electoral lists regarding regions, provinces and provincial-capital municipalities pertains to the related political councils. (FDS 2010, Article 4)

Lastly, FDS promotes four forums (for the elaboration of the party manifesto) that are always open to outside contributions: on labour, on democracy, on migrants and a general one.

SEL, as opposed to FDS, is structured around the undisputed leadership of Nichi Vendola, who was elected president unanimously. With respect to the office of president, the statute of SEL states that the president 'exercises his functions on the basis of the document approved at the moment of his election at the national convention' (SEL 2011, Article 3). The national convention also elects the national assembly, and the latter in turn elects the national presidency (another body of political orientation) and the national coordinating body (with executive functions). As for the rest, the organisation of SEL follows a traditional model, with federations at provincial and regional levels and with 'circles' at local levels. The activities of these circles are open to non-members, who, however, do not have voting rights (without exceptions). With respect to the relationships between elected officials and the party organisation, the differences from FDS are marginal. On the candidate selection process, the SEL statute is, however, a little vague, although its recent modifications (October 2011) have highlighted more clearly the will of the party to adopt forms of participatory democracy, including primaries. This issue deserves a comment.

SEL was born thanks to a leader who was able to emerge onto the national political scene through his participation in coalition primary elections. The ability to use such a tool to its advantage is at the basis of a good portion of SEL's political success. Indeed, Vendola's party was able to select candidates capable not only of winning coalition primaries but of winning actual elections as well. This occurred in the elections for the mayoralties of Milan and Cagliari in 2011 and of Genoa in 2012.

To analyse participatory linkage, it is useful to highlight three additional characteristics that differentiate SEL from FDS:

1. The value attributed to meetings and study and research activities (open also to non-members) for producing political ideas and proposals. For example, Article 1 of the statute states that SEL 'promotes moments of collective training, such as seminars and study sessions' to further develop its party governing bodies. In addition to promoting the establishment of thematic forums within the national assembly, open also to non-members (a similar rule applies in the FDS), the statute also calls for the establishment of a scientific committee responsible for policies. It is notable that the meetings promoted by SEL's scientific committee (contrary to the practice of the scientific committee of the FDS) are numerous, spread widely throughout the country and well advertised over the Web.
2. The emphasis given to the use of the Web, not only as a tool for promoting the party, but as a means of information and participation as well. Article 1 of SEL's Statute further states,

> SEL guarantees information, transparency and participation. To this end, in addition to the direct participation of the members and the circles, it will exploit the Web Information System (SIW), also to test the new forms of digital democracy. (SEL 2011, Article 1)

Moreover, the local circles of SEL are required to create websites and to use them to disseminate information on their activities and initiatives, contact information, political documents and press releases (Article 8). SEL, in fact, sees the internet also as a tool for communication between leadership and voters. It is no coincidence that Vendola is the most cited Italian political leader on the Web nowadays. On Facebook, he currently counts 524,738 fans and he is the European politician with the most fans in Europe (Vaccari 2012).

3. The presence within SEL of ground-level structures that are parallel to and independent of the party organisation: the so-called 'Nichi's factories'. Nichi's factories were first created in Apulia in 2009 as local electoral committees in support of the candidacy of Nichi Vendola in both the primaries and the regional elections of 2010. Over time, however, these mutated into outright 'online support circles', crossing regional boundaries (Cramarossa 2011). Today they can be considered consultation and communication sites for the leader, a

means that Vendola uses to establish direct linkage with his supporters (Poguntke 2002, p. 45).

The leadership and the organisational structure of FDS and SEL are supported and accepted by their middle-level elites in the sense that the national delegates who were interviewed declared that they were satisfied on the whole with the characteristics of their organisations.

Asked to indicate the most important features of their party, 47 per cent of SEL delegates selected the 'charismatic leadership of Vendola' as their first choice and an additional 24 per cent selected this response as their second choice. The other characteristic most selected by middle-level elites of SEL is the 'the presence of various political and cultural areas within the party' (31 per cent selected this as their first choice and an additional 25 per cent as their second). Moreover, it is noteworthy that merely 15 per cent of the middle-level elites wished to transform SEL into a federation of parties, and also that, in answering a different question, 61 per cent agreed that the success of SEL was due solely to Vendola.

Within FDS, however, 64 per cent of delegates were convinced that a collective leadership was a resource for the party, even though a similar percentage of respondents wished to transform FDS into a full-blown party. Also noteworthy in this regard are the opinions expressed by each of the two groups of delegates regarding the other party. Despite their openness towards the possibility of electoral alliances with the other party, supported by over 50 per cent of the two samples, 41 per cent of the SEL middle-level elite considered FDS unable to truly grasp society's real needs, whereas a similar percentage of FDS respondents believed that SEL was an excessively personalised party.

The centralisation of candidacies is not considered a 'very' or a 'fairly significant' issue by more than 55 per cent of SEL delegates and by approximately 60 per cent of FDS delegates. However, the question 'What criterion should your party follow in choosing candidates?' does reveal some dissatisfaction within Vendola's party. In FDS, 56 per cent of the respondents thought that candidates should be selected by the 'governing bodies of the party' (and a mere 37 per cent preferred the primaries), whereas over 90 per cent of SEL delegates desired primaries (and, of these, 54 per cent preferred primaries open to non-members).

The greater propensity of SEL delegates to adopt a bottom-up logic in the choice of candidacies is also evident in the answers to the question 'At what level should the choice of the candidates in the districts take place?' Fifty-eight per cent of SEL respondents (compared with 45 per cent of FDS respondents) answered that it should be at a local level, an additional 35 per cent said at a regional level (compared with 30 per cent of FDS delegates) and a mere seven per cent chose the national level (compared with 25 per cent of FDS respondents).

Conversely, one finds widespread satisfaction in both parties regarding the role of national conventions (with percentages that vary between 60 and 80 per cent of delegates) for settling internal conflicts and for putting party officials in touch with the party on the ground.

SEL delegates, therefore, aspire to a party with strong charismatic leadership, yet one deeply democratic within. FDS delegates, instead, are bound to the idea of a traditional party that rejects the personalisation of politics, but with a strong structure capable of disentangling internal conflicts. The latter goal is not easily achieved in a federated structure with strong and differentiated identities.

Summarising, FDS has a traditional organisational structure, resembling closely that of a substantially hierarchical and centralised mass party, opposed to the personalisation of politics. Members exercise their right to vote at the various organisational levels, electing their representatives. Relationships of members with the leadership are mainly indirect, mediated by the FDS's founding organisations. SEL differs from FDS especially in the commitment shown to involving its members (and non-members) in defining its political agenda. This takes place, in particular, through meetings, forums and the events organised by the scientific committee.

Environmental Linkage: Relationships with Social Movements and Organised Civil Society

Environmental linkage is that part of the party linkage process that deals with the relationships that the parties establish with interest groups and with organised civil society (Lawson 1980). In this section, I show how SEL and FDS form connections with social groups, labour unions and social organisations, using the analysis of the opinions and attitudes of their middle-level elites as a starting point. On the one hand, I analyse the participation of delegates in various public events, associations and social groups, in the belief that these links are a means through which a party can integrate the issues flagged up by organisations of civil society. On the other, I examine the type of political relationships that the two parties intend to shape with labour unions and social movements.

As national party delegates, the respondents of SEL and FDS are very active not only in the more traditional forms of political participation but also in less conventional ones such as occupation of public buildings or boycotts. SEL delegates distinguish themselves by using methods of political participation that could be termed 'of a new generation'—I refer, for example, not only to email bombings (forms of cyber-attack) but also to involvement in 'creative' events such as flash mobs (attended at least once by one-third of the younger SEL delegates)—whereas FDS delegates seem to feel more confident with more traditional forms of participation.

In recent events (demonstrations in support of FIOM[7] on 16 October 2010 and the No-Berlusconi Day on 5 December 2009), the participation rates of FDS delegates were 30–35 percentage points greater than those of SEL delegates. Significant differences emerge when a demonstration deals with labour issues, with the North Atlantic Treaty Organisation (NATO) and with the institutions of international capitalism (G8, International Monetary Fund [IMF], World Trade Organisation

[WTO]). The attachment of FDS delegates to this form of participation and their propensity to establish a direct experiential relation with those citizens (and potential voters) who support the issues championed by the party are notable. But how much of this propensity translates into a more organised presence on the ground? And, most of all, how much of it is transformed into closer links to civil society and social movements?

Compared with SEL, FDS has a local structure with deeper roots, not only because FDS—as we mentioned before—was born from the union of two associations (March 23 Labour and Solidarity and Socialism 2000) and of two associations (Labour and Solidarity and Socialism 2000) and of two parties that have been present—and independent—within the Italian party system for ten (PDCI) and 20 (PRC) years, respectively. Not only that, but PRC and PDCI are, respectively, a direct child and a direct grandchild of the old PCI and, as such, have inherited part of its organisational structure. This legacy (which has nothing to do with the legacy received by PDS–DS, today's PD) is certainly a primary resource for the survival of FDS, but it is also a limitation upon organisational innovation. At this level, what differentiates the two parties is the use of the internet. Websites and social networks are much more important in the organisation of SEL than in that of FDS, and this constitutes a valuable potentiality and a fundamental means of organisational diversification. As shown in Table 1, 78 per cent of SEL delegates consider party websites an important tool for recruiting members (the difference in opinion compared with FDS delegates exceeds 50 percentage points); 85 per cent consider them a crucial means for communicating with the electorate (28 percentage points more than FDS); 94 per cent consider them a necessary means for disseminating the political programme (20 percentage points more than FDS); and 90 per cent consider them fundamental for internal communication (18 percentage points more than FDS). The results relating to the use of social networks do not differ very much. In this case, the differences between the two parties (still in favour of SEL) vary from 34 to 14 percentage points. It goes without saying that the different relevance of the Web in the two parties for relations with the electorate can be linked to their other traits. First of all, the presence in SEL of a charismatic leader; second, the different appeal that SEL and FDS exert on younger, more social-network-literate generations. Indeed, it is precisely the presence of a charismatic leader that makes it easier to attract the attention of voters through the media, while the greater familiarity of SEL's sympathisers with the Web makes gathering and requesting information about the party quite a bit easier.

Let us return to the methods of participation in the network of civil society associations. Up to the 1980s, the PCI possessed a deeply rooted organisational structure (there was at least one local branch of the party in almost every one of the more than 8,000 Italian municipalities), which was connected, after the end of World War II, to a multi-faceted network of associations. It represented, above all in the 'red regions' (Emilia Romagna, Tuscany, Umbria, Marche), the reference point of political and social life. The ideological vote guaranteed to the PCI not only stable electoral performances, but stable control over a large network of associations, ensuring

Table 1 Degree of importance of websites and social networks in relation to a series of activities

How important are websites for your party for ... ?	FDS (very + fairly important, %)	SEL (very + fairly important, %)	Difference between FDS and SEL (percentage points)
Recruiting members	27	78	−51*
Keeping contact with other European parties of the same family	40	48	−8
Disseminating the political programme	74	94	−20*
Internal communication	72	90	−18*
Communicating with the electorate	57	85	−28*
Total observations (*N*)	259	385	
How important are social networks for your party for ... ?	**FDS (very + fairly important, %)**	**SEL (very + fairly important, %)**	**Difference between FDS and SEL (percentage points)**
Recruiting members	30	64	−34*
Communicating with the electorate	51	78	−27*
Communicating with supporters	70	93	−23*
Disseminating the political programme	63	86	−23*
Publicising party events	78	92	−14*
Awareness campaigns on specific issues	78	93	−15*
Total observations (*N*)	259	385	

*Chi-squared test significant at a level of $p < 0.001$.
Source: Calculated from Bordandini and Di Virgilio (forthcoming).

efficient management of local administrations. The involvement in associations was also the means by which the PCI conveyed its system of beliefs and strengthened social cohesion at a local level. Thus, the PCI positioned itself at the centre of a multifarious network of associations (recreational, sporting, welfare, labour and professional) that it controlled more or less directly and to which it conferred identity and a sense of belonging (Cartocci 2011; Trigilia 1986).

After its name was changed, the associations linked to the old PCI began the slow process of gaining their autonomy from its successors (in particular from the PDS–DS, which had taken on the functions of the PCI at the local political level), losing in part their role as agents of political socialisation in local communities. Recreational and cultural associations regained their functions as circles for meetings and assemblies (increasingly for older people) with premises to lend to left and centre-left parties; labour unions—increasingly disorientated—strengthened their function as service agencies for members instead. Within the network of associations, the successors of the PCI (particularly PDS–DS), unable to dispense any further identity resources, could only play the role defined by their function: political interlocutor as representative of local government.

In this framework, we should not be surprised by the widespread awareness within the two parties of the radical left—in particular within FDS—of the need to resume contact with society. This was stated by 73 per cent of FDS respondents and by 67 per cent of those of SEL. Let us examine in detail the degree of participation of SEL and FDS in a series of associations present in civil society (Table 2).

Participation in the network of cultural and recreational associations—which could be defined as subcultural—does not reveal substantial differences between the two parties. It should be noted, however, that FDS shows a greater presence in labour and professional organisations. This is a significant difference (the difference between SEL and FDS is 14 percentage points with respect to members and 11 with respect to active participants), given that both parties place labour issues at the centre of their respective programmes. On the other hand, SEL differs from FDS in its relatively greater contact with civil society through secular volunteer work (with respect to active members, the difference exceeds ten per cent) and involvement in environmental associations (SEL has ten per cent more members among its delegates than FDS).

Therefore, FDS—as a Marxist party focused on labour issues—exhibits stronger ties to and a more active presence in labour unions, whereas SEL is more involved in associations that are not directly linked to economic issues. In this context, it is also interesting to note the delegates' answer to the question 'Should the party foster a privileged relationship with CGIL?' Forty-one per cent of FDS respondents, compared with 29 per cent of SEL delegates, said they 'strongly' agreed. Rather than having a privileged relationship with a specific labour union, SEL is focused on the reconsolidation of union unity. This preference is expressed by 82 per cent of SEL delegates, compared with 59 per cent of those of FDS. Thus, SEL delegates describe their party as an organisation that is willing to overturn the logic of the traditional radical left, opting for a bond that is less exclusive and less clearly identified with a left-wing union.

Very similar, on the other hand, are the positions of the two parties with respect to movements. Eighty-four per cent of FDS and 94 per cent of SEL delegates affirm that their party should establish a privileged relationship with movements. Within the two parties the positions with respect to movements are further divided into those who believe that the party should 'champion their issues' (47 per cent for FDS and 48 per cent for SEL) and those who believe the party should limit itself to 'acknowledge some of their requests' (48 per cent for FDS and 52 per cent for SEL). Lastly, there are five per cent of FDS delegates who are convinced that the party should consider the movements to be 'temporary protests'. Accordingly, in terms of attitudes towards movements, the data show a clear openness in both parties, even though this is slightly greater in Vendola's party. After all, both SEL and FDS are children of the PRC, which, from the end of the 1990s onwards, integrated the demands of the global justice movement into their own programmes. Over 70 per cent of respondents stated that they had their first political experiences and defined their political orientation within social movements.

In summary, it can be said that, in line with the parties of the European radical left, SEL and FDS—just like, before them, PDCI and PRC—aim to rebuild those ties to

Table 2 Membership and participation in a series of associations

Are you a member of and do you participate in the following associations?	FDS delegates ($N = 259$)		SEL delegates ($N = 385$)		Difference FDS – SEL: Membership (percentage points)	Difference FDS – SEL participation (percentage points)
	% members	% members who participate actively	% members	% members who participate actively		
Labour and professional	74	51	60	40	14*	11*
Cultural and recreational	79	54	79	54	0	0
Secular volunteer	43	28	50	38	− 7**	− 10**
Religious volunteer	3	2	5	4	− 2	− 2
Environmental	42	26	52	31	− 10**	− 5**

*$p < 0.001$; **$p < 0.01$.
Source: Calculated from Bordandini and Di Virgilio (forthcoming).

organised civil society, which the transformation of mass parties into electoral and professional machines helped to break.

This process of reconciliation with unions and social groups involves both parties. Party targets and primary interlocutors, however, are different. FDS seeks a closer and more defined link to labour unions. It seems to aim at relaunching a symbiotic relationship similar to that which characterised the PCI and the CGIL (see note 7) in the 1970s (Mattina 2010; Morlino 1998). This attempt is perhaps unrealistic, but not surprising, considering the Marxist terminology with which the FDS statute addresses the labour issue: 'FDS struggles to overcome capitalist and class supremacy ... for the liberation of labour from exploitation, for labour rights and for the right to work' (FDS 2010, p. 1).

The protection of workers is a central theme for SEL as well. The emphasis, however, is different and one observes a greater openness towards social movements and new social networks: from fair trade economy to 'happy de-growth'. In this sense, SEL presents itself as a pluralist party, open to ground-level labour union committees (*comitati di base* [COBAS]) and to the manifold associations present in civil society, but without the intention of establishing privileged relationships with them.

Conclusions

This paper's objective was to analyse the two main parties of the Italian radical left—with respect to the organisational structure suggested by their statutes and to the methods they employ to keep in contact with members, voters and organised civil society—in order to capture their similarities and differences. This was carried out mainly from the point of view of their middle-level elites.

In terms of the construction of participatory and environmental linkages, the differences between the two parties are related, on the one hand, to the history and to the degree of factionalism that defines them and, on the other, to their organisational structure and the characteristics of their leaderships.

At the organisational level, FDS is founded on collective leadership, a traditional structure with provincial and regional federations, grassroots 'houses of the left' and workers' circles. Its statute strongly protects the parity of the associated components in order to keep the internal balances unchanged and to prevent the emergence of a single leader. Within this framework, it is not surprising that FDS encourages relationships between members and party leaders that are structured, hierarchical and based on the intermediation of elected middle-level officials. Also with respect to the relationships between party leaders and voters, FDS, on the one hand, rejects any kind of personalisation of politics and, on the other, promotes the reactivation of traditional links to collateral organisations, labour unions above all. In Poguntke's terms (2002), organisational linkage prevails in the FDS.

SEL, on the other hand, sees its strength in the charismatic leadership of Nichi Vendola, in his ability to involve younger generations and to garner visibility through the media and the use of the Web. His ability to exploit the Web and the media constitutes an important resource for the party and a very innovative aspect of his political action. Creating and updating websites is promoted by statute, as is experimenting with forms of participatory and digital democracy. It is no coincidence that SEL delegates attribute far more importance to party websites and social networks than do FDS delegates. They see their relevance not only for disseminating SEL's political programme, but for internal and external communication (with voters, members and supporters) and for recruiting members as well. Not only does a direct linkage between party leadership and voters prevail in SEL, but the party also demonstrates a greater inclination towards bottom-up logic and the direct involvement of individuals in the party decision-making process.

FDS, therefore, appears to be the latest attempt to revive a party model and a system of traditional beliefs that have led in recent years to the emergence of profound contradictions, electoral defeats and splits. From this perspective, FDS seems trapped in a time warp, not only with respect to its electoral pool, but also in relation to its proposed organisational model. Its relationships with civil society combine traditional modes of interaction, which contain the classical references to communist subculture, with more innovative ties to social movements. However, although the agenda set forth by social movements—based on global justice, pacifist, environmental and libertarian issues—has become part of its system of beliefs, the priority of FDS remains the defence of the communist identity. Thus, this party not only attempts to combine a traditional organisational structure with an ideological project oriented towards reviving belief systems of the past, but also tends to incorporate social movement issues as well. One could speak of a mass and 'movementist' party.

SEL presents itself as a new type of party, based essentially—in line with the many and diverse party experiences of the past 15 years—on the concept of a 'personal party' (Calise 2010) or, at least, of a highly personalised one that places (in addition to workers' rights) the issues of a new generation at the centre of its political discourse, that uses new communication tools, that supports an open and pluralist vision of centre-left alignment and that, consequently, is open to the compromises required by membership in a coalition. In this manner, it has overcome many of the causes of the fractures sustained by the Italian radical left and centre-left in the past (1998, 2008), since it no longer considers government an inevitable evil. And this is even more evident if one considers SEL's current constructively critical attitude regarding the reforms of the second non-political Italian government, formed in November 2011: the Monti government. SEL has a less radical attitude than FDS—the latter party is hardly mentioned in the Italian media—and especially compared with Di Pietro's Italia dei Valori (Italy of Values, IDV). SEL is, therefore, a party of the radical left which is both capable of not obstructing a caretaker government and adept in identifying and supporting winning candidates in coalition primaries for local elections; an 'electoral-professional party' capable of proposing its own leader (Nichi Vendola) as candidate for the premiership of the center-left coalition in primary elections.

But which of the two party models, and of the party linkages, of the Italian radical left is best suited to the competitive Italian arena? In the 2009 European elections the two parties each obtained around three per cent of the vote while adopting the same coalition strategy for the parliamentary elections. It is an undisputed fact, however, that FDS and SEL are performing very divergent roles in the local and national political scene. The influence of SEL at an institutional level is much broader than that of FDS. SEL is at the head of important regional and local governments due to a series of circumstances relating mainly to its ability to 'take over' the coalition primaries organised by the PD. This is not just a fortunate coincidence, but a result obtained by the party thanks to its innovative political message and to its ability to shape favourable political situations, select winning candidates and support them through electoral contests—abilities that should be analysed appropriately through specific research, but that are undoubtedly connected to the party linkage modes proposed by Vendola's party.

Acknowledgements

I would like to thank Roberto Cartocci, Aldo Di Virgilio, Marco Lisi and Myrto Tsakatika, as well as the two anonymous referees, for their useful suggestions and comments.

Notes

[1] The research project gathered a total of 5,714 responses of national party delegates within the context of 21 national conventions (of 18 different parties) that took place between 2004 and 2010. The surveys were coordinated by Paola Bordandini and Aldo Di Virgilio (Department of Political Science, University of Bologna) and financed by a multi-year Progetto di Ricerca di Interesse Nazionale (National Interest Research Project, PRIN) that involved the Universities of Bologna, Cosenza, Florence and Trieste. Data collection was carried out by means of a structured self-completion questionnaire distributed during the conventions. The questionnaires consisted of a general part in common to all parties and of a specific part adapted to the characteristics of each party and to the context in which the convention took place.

[2] The confidence intervals and the chi-squared tests in the tables have been included solely for completeness. They lose, in fact, most of their explicative ability because the data were not generated by means of random sampling.

[3] For the transformation of the organisational and ideological structure of PCI/PDS/DS/PD, refer to the works of Ignazi (1992), Baccetti (1997), Bordandini, Di Virgilio and Raniolo (2008) and Pasquino (2009). For the political and the organisational history of the PRC, see Bertolino (2004) and Mulé (2009).

[4] The birth of the new PD in autumn 2007 was based on a political and strategic innovation: refusal of electoral agreements with the radical left. Regarding the causes and the consequences of this innovation implemented by Walter Veltroni, see Di Virgilio (2010).

[5] The electoral law contained a strong incentive to present a single list instead of a coalition of parties, since it established a threshold of four per cent in the case of single parties or eight per cent for electoral coalitions. This choice required the single parties to abandon their symbols, including the traditional hammer and sickle.

[6] Vendola himself prevailed twice (2005 and 2010) in the coalition primaries held to choose the centre-left candidate for governor of Apulia, and won both elections.

[7] Italy has traditionally had three labour unions: Confederazione Generale Italiana del Lavoro (Italian General Confederation of Labour, CGIL), identified in the past with the old PCI and today with the left and centre-left parties; Confederazione Italiana Sindacati Lavoratori (Italian Confederation of Workers' Unions, CISL), with a Catholic orientation; Unione Italiana del Lavoro (Italian Labour Union, UIL), with a centrist orientation. Federazione Impiegati Operai Metallurgici (Federation of Metalworkers, FIOM) is the labour union of the Italian metalworkers associated with CGIL and has constituted, in recent years, the hard-line wing of the Italian unions.

References

Baccetti, C. (1997) *Il PDS. Verso un nuovo modello di partito?* Il Mulino, Bologna.

Bertolino, S. (2004) *Rifondazione Comunista*, Il Mulino, Bologna.

Bordandini, P. & Di Virgilio, A. (2007) 'Comunisti Italiani. Ritratto di un partito di nicchia', *Rivista Italiana di Scienza Politica*, vol. 37, no. 2, pp. 261–296.

Bordandini, P. & Di Virgilio, A. (forthcoming) *Delegati di partito. SEL e FDS*, Clueb, Bologna.

Bordandini, P., Di Virgilio, A. & Mulè, R. (eds) (2011) 'I delegati congressuali di partito', in *Polis*, vol. 25, no. 2, special issue.

Bordandini, P., Di Virgilio, A. & Raniolo, F. (2008) 'The birth of a party: the case of the Italian Partito Democratico', *South European Society & Politics*, vol. 13, no. 3, pp. 303–324.

Bosco, A. (2000) *Comunisti. Trasformazioni di partito in Italia, Spagna e Portogallo*, Il Mulino, Bologna.

Bosco, A. (2001) 'Four actors in search of a role: the Southern European Communist parties', in *Parties, Politics and Democracy in the New Southern Europe*, eds N. Diamandouros & R. Gunther, Johns Hopkins University Press, Baltimore, pp. 329–387.

Botella, J. & Ramiro, L. (eds) (2003) *The Crisis of Communism and Party Change: The Evolution of Western European Communist and Post-Communist Parties*, ICPS, Barcelona.

Calise, M. (2010) *Il Partito personale. I due corpi del leader*, Laterza, Bari.

Cartocci, R. (2011) 'Political culture', in *International Encyclopedia of Political Science*, eds B. Badie, D. Berg-Schlosser & L. Morlino, Sage, London, pp. 1968–1980.

Cramarossa, V. (ed.) (2011) *C'è un'Italia migliore. Nichi Vendola e le fabbriche di Nichi*, Fandango, Rome.

Di Virgilio, A. (2010) 'Cambiare strategia a regole invariate. La rivoluzione dell'offerta', in *Proporzionale se vi pare*, eds R. D'Alimonte & A. Chiaromonte, Il Mulino, Bologna, pp. 33–73.

FDS (2010) 'Statuto della Federazione della Sinistra', available online at: http://www.federazionedellasinistra.com/federazione/?page_id=7 (accessed 20 October 2012)

Heidar, K. & Saglie, J. (2003a) 'A decline of linkage? Intra-party participation in Norway, 1991–2000', *European Journal of Political Research*, vol. 42, no. 6, pp. 761–786.

Heidar, K. & Saglie, J. (2003b) 'Predestined parties? Organizational change in Norwegian political parties', *Party Politics*, vol. 9, no. 2, pp. 219–239.

Ignazi, P. (1992) *Dal PCI al PDS*, Il Mulino, Bologna.

Katz, R.S. & Mair, P. (1995) 'Changing models of party organization and party democracy: the emergence of the cartel party', *Party Politics*, vol. 1, no. 1, pp. 5–28.

Lawson, K. (ed.) (1980) *Political Parties and Linkage: A Comparative Perspective*, Yale University Press, New Haven.

March, L. (2011) *Radical Left Parties in Europe*, Routledge, New York.

Mattina, L. (2010) *I gruppi di interesse*, Il Mulino, Bologna.

Morlino, L. (1998) *Democracy between Consolidation and Crisis: Parties, Groups, and Citizens in Southern Europe*, Oxford University Press, Oxford.

Mulé, R. (2009) *Il popolo di Rifondazione Comunista: Storia, opinioni, atteggiamenti*, Carocci, Rome.
Pasquino, G. (ed.) (2009) *Il Partito Democratico. Elezione del segretario, organizzazione e potere*, Bononia University Press, Bologna.
Poguntke, T. (2002) 'Parties without firm social roots? Party organisational linkage', in *Political Parties in the New Europe: Political and Analytical Challenges*, eds KR Luther & F. Müller-Rommel, Oxford University Press, Oxford, pp. 43–62.
Römmele, A., Farrell, D. & Ignazi, P. (eds) (2005) *Political Parties and Political Systems: The Concept of Linkage Revisited*, Greenwood/Praeger, Westport, CT.
SEL (2011) *Statuto approvato dall'Assemblea nazionale del 8 ottobre 2011*, available online at: http://www.sinistraecologialiberta.it/statuto/ (accessed 20 October 2012)
Trigilia, C. (1986) *Grandi partiti e piccole imprese*, Il Mulino, Bologna.
Vaccari, C. (2012) *La Politica Online: Internet, partiti e cittadini nelle democrazie occidentali*, Il Mulino, Bologna.

Paola Bordandini is an Assistant Professor in the Department of Political and Social Science, University of Bologna, where she teaches methodology of political science. She co-authored 'The birth of a party: the case of the Italian Partito Democratico' (*South European Society and Politics*, 2008). Recently, she has co-edited a special issue on Italian party delegates, 'I Delegati Congressuali di Partito' (*Polis*, 2011).

The Radical Left's Turn towards Civil Society in Greece: One Strategy, Two Paths

Myrto Tsakatika and Costas Eleftheriou

The Communist Party of Greece (KKE) and the Coalition of the Radical Left (SYRIZA) made remarkable 'turns towards civil society' over the last decade. It is argued that this was primarily a response aimed at strengthening their social legitimacy, which had reached its lowest point in the early 1990s. Differences in the way the two parties attempted to stabilise and engage their membership and re-establish links to trade unions and new social movements can be attributed to their distinct ideological and organisational legacies. Despite those differences, their respective linkage strategies were both successful until the game-changing 2012 Greek national elections, which brought about the remarkable rise of SYRIZA and the electoral demise of the KKE.

Kay Lawson's seminal work treated political parties as two-way mediating mechanisms that link the preferences of citizens to the political process (Lawson 1980). The contemporary study of party change has documented a notable weakening of those links over recent decades. Social and technological change has triggered a process of party adaptation whereby parties principally rely on media campaigns and state funding to ensure their electoral survival (Katz & Mair 1995), not on the mobilisation of their own partisans (Dalton & Wattenberg 2000). Furthermore, given that parties need flexibility to respond to social change by broadening their appeal and diversifying their programmatic offer, they have distanced themselves from trade unions and other organisations of civil society (Allern & Bale 2012). Linkage has thus been assumed to have fallen lower in the list of parties' priorities. This state of affairs may not necessarily threaten mainstream parties' electoral survival, but it may place their legitimacy in question to the extent that they are perceived to have turned their backs on their grassroots.

Radical left parties' legitimacy can be argued to be more dependent on the pursuit of linkage than the legitimacy of mainstream catch-all parties. This is because their core ideology is closely connected to notions of social representation: whether they come from a communist tradition that conceptualises the party as a representative of working class interests, or a left-libertarian tradition that emphasises notions of internal party democracy and bottom-up participation (Kitschelt 1988), radical left parties must be shown to actively maintain close links to their social constituency if they are to justify their raison d'être. Government participation, an option that radical left parties have been taking up more frequently in recent years (Bale & Dunphy 2011), can be argued to strengthen perceptions that these parties have distanced themselves from their particular social constituency. This is because being part of a coalition government increases the probability of a radical left party agreeing to measures and policies its grassroots would not choose. Furthermore, because they start from a weaker electoral position than mainstream parties (March 2011), their electoral survival may also be at risk if their legitimacy is weakened. This predicament may well be expected to make linkage a matter of higher priority for radical left parties. The more the legitimacy of radical parties is in question, the more we can expect them to pursue linkage, adapting their organisational routines and programmatic offer to suit that purpose. The way they do so can be expected to be much more dependent on their past ideological and institutional trajectories precisely because they are parties whose legitimacy inherently depends on ideological consistency and representation of, or active engagement with, a *particular* social or political constituency.

At the turn of the twenty-first century, the two established parties of the Greek radical left, the Κομμουνιστικό Κόμμα Ελλάδος (Communist Party of Greece, KKE) and the Συνασπισμός της Αριστεράς, της Οικολογίας και των Κινημάτων (Coalition of the Left, Ecology and Social Movements, SYN) made a remarkable 'turn towards civil society', reflected in an attempt to consolidate their membership base and renew their cadre pool; a marked reinvestment was made in creating 'microcosms' that link their broader electorate to the party, as well as a visible effort to reconfirm existing links and forge new links to trade unions and social movements. Despite this common strategic shift towards reprioritising linkage, there are pronounced differences both in terms of how the two parties have pursued this strategy and the implications this has had for their own organisational development and electoral fortunes.

The next section will set out the context within which the two parties of the Greek radical left have reprioritised linkage and explore the factors that explain this development. We expect to find that the parties of the Greek left invested in linkage in response to a weakening of their legitimacy. The two following sections will look at what KKE's and SYN's 'turn towards civil society' has meant for the way they articulate their appeal to particular social constituencies, their participatory linkages and their environmental linkage, particularly in what concerns trade unions and social movements. We expect to find that ideological and institutional legacy will explain differences between the two parties. The final section will focus on the two parties' linkage strategies during the economic crisis.

Relevant data have been gathered by examining party statutes, congress documents and statements in the party press and conducting nine semi-structured interviews over 2011 with leading cadres of the KKE, SYN and their youth wings, trade unionists and representatives of social movements affiliated or otherwise related to the two parties of the Greek radical left.

The Greek Radical Left's Turn towards Civil Society

The history of the Greek radical left is marked by a bitter division (February 1968) inside the KKE and the subsequent establishment of the Κομμουνιστικό Κόμμα Ελλάδος Εσωτερικού (Communist Party of Greece of the Interior, KKE-es) by expelled cadres. The origins of the split lay in the different positions taken on the KKE's political direction and organisational strategy, respectively by the party cadres that operated illegally inside Greece and those in exile in Eastern Europe (Kapetanyannis 1979) before and during the military dictatorship (1967–74). The former were in favour of an open mass party organisation based on a broad political coalition that would extend beyond communist forces, while the latter insisted on preserving the party's Marxist–Leninist characteristics. The split became final after the August 1968 Soviet invasion of Prague, when the cadres of the Interior took a critical stance against the invasion, while those of the KKE remained loyal to Moscow (Clogg 1987, p. 177). After the transition to democracy in 1974, KKE and KKE-es followed two different political trajectories, respectively 'orthodox' and Eurocommunist (Kalyvas & Marantzidis 2002), the former being consistently more successful than the latter in electoral terms. However, the warring comrades joined forces again in 1988 (Verney 1989). International and national developments were favourable to this rapprochement.

Gorbachev's 'perestroika' had allowed a softening of the lines of division and a large section of the younger cadres of the KKE was in search of a new direction that would involve internal democratisation, programmatic renewal and an opening to new issues, such as the environment and gender equality, a direction that the KKE-es had already taken some time before. On the domestic front, the left's social democratic competitor, Πανελλήνιο Σοσιαλιστικό Κίνημα (Panhellenic Socialist Movement, PASOK), lay in tatters. The socialist Prime Minister Andreas Papandreou and his key associates were under accusation of scandal, which involved party funding from illicit sources and revealed the extensive clientelistic linkages between business interests and politics which had been built up under PASOK's eight-year rule. Leadership in both parties of the radical left saw an opportunity for cooperation against a formidable common enemy caught in a moment of weakness (Kapetanyannis 1993). In the eyes of the two parties' elites, PASOK was the main benefactor of post-1974 radicalisation and an exploiter of the left's discourse, social base and political tradition.

It was these factors that led to the formation of the electoral Συνασπισμός της Αριστεράς και της Προόδου (Coalition of the Left and Progress) which contested three national elections (June 1989, November 1989, 1990) (Table 1) and participated in an unlikely government alliance with the mainstream centre-right party Νέα Δημοκρατία (New Democracy, ND) under the premiership of Tzannis Tzannetakis (Pridham & Verney 1991). The government's official purpose was to send the former prime minister to trial and impose a clean-up of the corrupt clientelistic politics of the time. The left's informal aim was to ensure that PASOK would no longer be able to form single-party governments.

This strategy was destructive for both parties of the radical left, but more so for the larger partner, the KKE. Since the political division between left and right which goes back to the Civil War (1946–49) remained deeply embedded in Greek political culture, leftist voters did not appreciate the decision of the left parties' leaderships to engage in government cooperation with the centre-right; moreover, the stated aim of the Tzannetakis government was not achieved: after a long judicial process there was ultimately very little 'cleaning up'. After the electoral downturn for the left in the 1990 national elections which saw the centre-right ND form a new single-party government, the KKE pulled out of the coalition and lost 40 per cent of its cadres after a major party split in the party's 13th Congress (February 1991) (Doukas 1991). The former coalition was re-established as a unified party, which included cadres from the former KKE-es and the breakaway 'modernising' cadres from the KKE.

In the first part of the 1990s, the Greek left as a whole was thus delegitimised in the eyes of its traditional electorate, bruised by participation in government with the centre-right and experienced internal strife and extensive demobilisation of party members, while the collapse of the Soviet Union (USSR) added an identity crisis to its woes. The extent to which the left's legitimacy had been damaged was only partially reflected in the drop of the two parties' aggregate vote share, evident in the second national election of 1989, and subsequently the elections that took place in 1990 and 1993 (Table 1).

Throughout the 1980s and early 1990s neither of the radical left parties, more in SYN's case and less so in the case of the KKE, shied away from office-seeking. This was evident in their accommodating stance towards PASOK trade unionists in the steering bodies of the official trade union confederations, at the level of local politics where both parties of the radical left often participated in governing coalitions with PASOK, as well as in their participation in the Tzannetakis government when the opportunity to contest PASOK's dominance of the centre-left emerged. Throughout this period, both parties invested their resources in local government, official trade union politics and during the Tzannetakis government in their parliamentary and ministerial presence. At the same time they neglected linkage, when it came both to their own members and to their links with their trade union grassroots and the new social movements. After the de-legitimisation suffered in the early 1990s, an office-seeking strategy was clearly no longer a viable option for either of the two radical left parties, which were now aiming for survival, in competition with PASOK and with each other,

Table 1 KKE and SYN Vote Shares (%) and Seats in National and European Elections

National elections	1989	1989	1990	1993	1996	2000	2004	2007	2009	2012 (May)	2012 (June)
KKE				4.5 (9)	5.6 (11)	5.5 (11)	5.9 (12)	8.1 (22)	7.5 (21)	8.5 (26)	4.5 (12)
	13.1 (28)	11 (21)	10.3 (19)								
SYN				2.9 (0)	5.1 (10)	3.2 (6)					
SYRIZA							3.3 (6)	5 (14)	4.6 (13)	16.8 (52)	26.9 (71)
European elections	1989				1994	1999	2004		2009		
KKE		6.3 (2)	8.7 (3)	9.5 (3)	8.3 (2)						
	14.3 (4)										
SYN		6.3 (2)	5.2 (2)								
SYRIZA				4.1 (1)	4.7 (1)						

Source: Greek Ministry of the Interior, available online at: http://www.ypes.gr/en/Elections
Notes: The 1989–90 national and 1989 European election results refer to Synaspismos as an electoral coalition. SYN took part in all national elections from 2004 onwards and in the 2009 European election as part of the SYRIZA coalition. All numbers in parentheses refer to parliamentary seats.

in what at the time seemed to be a limited electoral space; their assessment was that they needed to reclaim their legitimacy before they could begin to raise their hopes about their electoral performance.

A new strategy was thus called for: they would need to rewire themselves in order to fulfil a protest role vis-à-vis the established party 'cartel', re-emphasise their ideology, distinct policies and principles and rearticulate their appeal to their traditional constituency. A key plank of their strategy involved a turn towards civil society, evident after the end of the 1990s, which included a reformulation of their social and programmatic appeal, a rearrangement of their internal organisation with the aim of preserving their membership levels and a pronounced investment in maintaining existing organisational links and establishing new links to trade unions and social movements.

The Communist Party of Greece (KKE)

The KKE is considered one of the most strictly 'orthodox' communist parties and basic trustees of the Soviet political and ideological tradition in Europe (March 2011, pp. 52–56). The party that rose from the ashes of the 1991 split achieved its political survival by mobilising core political and ideological resources from its political tradition, engaging in a process that could be described as an organisational and programmatic 'rebolshevisation' (Eleftheriou, forthcoming). The party's 'dominant coalition' interpreted the post-1991 political environment as extremely hostile to the KKE and implemented an introvert, yet aggressive, party strategy whose aim has been the formation of a cohesive electoral and membership base. It was that cohesion which in the leadership's view would ensure the party's survival.

A basic programmatic trait of the KKE since the mid-1990s has been the pursuit of an 'anti-imperialist anti-monopoly democratic front of struggle' (KKE 1996a), a social coalition that is the precondition for the construction of a political front and is meant to function as a stepping stone for the transition to socialism. The party's priority, in other words, is to construct strong ties with the working class and other 'popular strata' such as the 'semi-proletarians, poor farmers and the most oppressed urban petty bourgeois strata' (KKE 1996a). The KKE's role is to direct these social forces to the fulfilment of the socialist prospect. Its organisation and ancillary structures are the basic channels of this strategy.

In terms of participatory linkage, the KKE as a Marxist–Leninist political party follows an extremely strict statute that defines its internal functioning. The present Statutes (KKE 1996b) were approved by the party's 15th Congress, which was pivotal for the KKE's subsequent development. The Statutes declare 'democratic centralism' to be the party's basic organisational principle (Article 9) and set out the centralised architecture of the party on a 'production-based' or 'territorial' basis (Article 13), pointing to the leading role of Central Committee and Political Bureau (Articles 14–33), mandating the creation of extraordinary 'party groups' in civil society organisations (Article 42) and setting the ground rules for communists' behaviour in public office (Article 43).

The KKE's aim is to consolidate a centralised and tightly controlled top-down party organisation, capable of recruiting and mobilising highly confident and determined members. To this end, the party maintains a strict method of recruitment which requires the candidate member to prove his or her merits in the 'political field' after being recommended to the party by two KKE members. The 1989–91 outbreak of internal dissent instilled a sense of self-preservation amongst the ranks of the KKE's new leadership, which linked party reconstruction to internal coherence. Factionalism is not tolerated and party purges of dissident voices have been known to occur. The KKE goes to great lengths to maintain secrecy regarding its membership levels and does not release official figures. Based on party funding data, Vernardakis estimates that the KKE had about 40,000 members in the early 1990s (2011, p. 76). Due to the Κομμουνιστική Νεολαία Ελλάδος (Communist Youth of Greece, KNE) enjoying an increase in membership since the late 1990s, and to judge from the visible strengthening of the KKE's presence in street demonstrations over the last decade, it can safely be assumed that the KKE's membership base has since grown. Unfortunately, data on the precise percentage of this increase are not available.

In practice, a very important organisational intervention that has taken place over the last decade has been the restructuring of the party's militant grassroots on a professional basis at the expense of the territorial principle. This change has had two main implications. First, the organisation's capacity as an electoral machine at local level has been greatly decreased. In national elections, the KKE is partly dependent upon labour-intensive campaigns; nevertheless, its communication strategies are highly centralised and its usage of new technologies and mass media—through the party's own newspaper and TV and radio stations—extensive. Second, the party's political action is predominantly oriented towards trade unions and workplaces; this means that party cadres are 'trained' to become union leaders or functionaries rather than public office holders.

In terms of the KKE's links to its ancillary structures, the most important development was the setting up of the Πανεργατικό Αγωνιστικό Μέτωπο (All Workers' Militant Front, PAME) in the late 1990s. In a context of diminishing union density[1] in the late 1990s and throughout the 2000s the marked increase in the number of precarious workers in Greece, especially among young people (Kretsos 2011), was a challenge for the Γενική Συνομοσπονδία Εργατών Ελλάδας (General Confederation of Greek Labour, GSEE)[2] as representative of the Greek workforce (Matsaganis 2007, pp. 541–545). The KKE's political rhetoric targeted these by and large non-unionised social groups, but the foundation of party cells in the new types of workplace was a difficult task. Moreover, the GSEE's dominance by mainstream political forces made it difficult for the KKE to pursue its own contentious political practices, which were in turn standing in the way of the party's political aims. At the time, it was felt that the KKE's longstanding ancillary organisation in the trade unions, the Ενιαία Συνδικαλιστική Αγωνιστική Κίνηση (Unified Trade Union Militant

Movement, ESAK), the aim of which is principally to present candidates for trade union elections at the confederate, federal and local level, was not up to the task at hand. It was therefore considered necessary for the KKE to explore new forms of intervention and mobilisation in the trade union movement. This need was addressed with the creation of PAME, founded on 3 April 1999.

In its constitution, PAME is described as 'an open, wide, uniting, democratic trade-union *front* of employees and workers, seeking to have in its lines the most vibrant, fighting forces of the working trade-union movement' (PAME 1999). In practice, PAME can be defined as a structure that aims to coordinate the activity of trade unions that are controlled by KKE members and cadres without being formally linked to the KKE. Despite the fact that PAME's leading cadres are also predominately KKE members, there are certain non-communist trade union cadres, defined as 'allies', that participate. The KKE's aim was to create a party-controlled quasi-trade-union organisation, with a centralised structure, but employing a looser recruitment logic. Although the KKE has always attempted to distinguish its own initiatives from PAME activity, the slogans and political positions were almost identical and many trade unionists affiliated to PAME were present at KKE marches or protests. It should be noted that PAME's collective bodies and secretariats are in close collaboration with the respective KKE Central Committee (CC) sections that deal with the documentation of the party's policy positions. Candidate selection for nearly all posts in PAME's secretariats and local committees is closely controlled by the CC, and in many cases CC sections and PAME secretariats have co-published policy papers.

The experience of PAME was extremely fruitful for the KKE's renewed tactics. In its first five years, PAME managed to consolidate its presence in many trade unions.[3] PAME's strength comes mainly from workers in the private sector, particularly construction, dock and textile workers, artists, typographers, hospital staff and employees in pharmaceutical companies. Where PAME does not control unions, either because the party's forces are a minority or in workplaces without any union representation, KKE members form 'militant committees'. A quasi-trade-union structure has thus taken shape to help workers who could not establish a union. PAME's organisational success has provoked criticism from the other wings of the trade union movement which are represented in GSEE and claim that the unity of the movement is threatened by PAME's mobilisation tactics. PAME has also considerably enhanced its contentious dynamics: during the 2000–07 period, strike hours increased from 384 to 672 hours per year in eight PAME-controlled trade union federations (Bithimitris 2008). Finally, PAME has been successfully used to serve the political aims of the KKE. For instance, PAME also started to mobilise its members for non-wage-related issues, as when it declared a 24-hour general strike against the Iraq War in 2003; PAME mobilises its followers in support of the KKE during electoral periods and many of its cadres are selected as candidate MPs, prefects, mayors, local councillors, etc.

The 17th Congress of the KKE (May 2005) identified PAME as the 'basic pole of clustering' for workers and other 'allying social strata' (KKE 2005). The increased share of votes gained by the party at the 2007 national elections (see Table 1) was essentially attributed to the successful presence of PAME in civil society and to the strengthening of KKE's influence in low-income areas (Vernardakis 2011, pp. 106–108). This meant that strengthening PAME was KKE's key priority. One of the organisational consequences has been that the PAME model was transferred to KNE's student wing, the Πανσπουδαστική Κίνηση Συνεργασίας (All Students' Movement of Cooperation, PKS)[4] with the formation of the 'Coordination Committee of Student Unions', a frontal structure that brought together unions and students close to PKS under central coordination and mirroring PAME's tactics in the student movement.

The relative success of KKE's top-down, vanguardist and sectarian approach put into practice through PAME can be attributed to the weakness of the official trade union confederations and the widespread perception that the latter were part and parcel of the corrupt, clientelistic system that has linked state and parties of government in Greece since the 1980s. PAME projected a well-organised, cohesive, combative and morally upright legitimising narrative, one that was designed to stand in stark contrast to the aforementioned flaws of the trade union 'establishment'. However, while the PAME approach has been effective in consolidating strong ties of support among a political subculture, in practice it has done little to establish significant environmental linkages understood as links to a broader array of social groups beyond its own ancillary structures.

The Coalition of the Left, Ecology and Social Movements (SYN) and the Coalition of the Radical Left (SYRIZA)

SYN, founded in 1992, defined itself as a pluralist left party of democratic socialism, neither orthodox communist nor social democratic, supporting a mixed economy and placing a fresh emphasis on 'new issues', particularly feminism, democratic rights and the environment (Kalyvas & Marantzidis 2002). SYN's original core consisted of cadres whose political origins lay in the party of the Ελληνική Αριστερά (Greek Left [EAR]) founded in 1987 (in turn established after the KKE-es leadership's decision to dissolve the party and contribute to the foundation of a non-communist left party) and a large group of dissidents who broke ranks with the KKE in 1991. It also incorporated a number of individuals and small groups coming from left social democracy, ecologism and the extra-parliamentary left, as well as independents.

The party's founding document appealed to 'the men and women of work and culture, the young and the excluded'. This was explicitly not a class appeal, since SYN effectively presented itself as a catch-all party throughout the 1990s, one that aimed to be present in 'every nook and cranny of Greek society'. There was also an explicit trans-class appeal to groups affected by gender inequality and environmental degradation (SYN 1992). In practice, most of its vote share, membership and cadres have mainly been from among the ranks of highly educated employees in the public sector, professionals and small employers (Vernardakis 2011, pp. 108–110, 296–298). However, as a result of changes in internal factional dynamics, with the radical, protest-oriented Αριστερό Ρεύμα (Left Current) faction displacing the more moderate (and sympathetic to government cooperation with PASOK) Ανανεωτική Πτέρυγα (Renewal Wing) in the party leadership after 2000 (Eleftheriou 2009), SYN shifted to a broadly defined class appeal aimed at targeting, primarily, younger cohorts and, secondarily, precariously employed workers in the services sector, social categories that were politically under-represented (SYN 2003).

In terms of participatory linkage SYN was meant to be a 'party of its members'. The statutes explicitly promoted members' direct participation in party policy-making, decision-making and candidate selection, giving extended powers to local branches. Sittings of the party's Central Political Committee (CPC) are open to members, as are the meetings of its departments, where party policy-making takes place and all interested members are invited to contribute. Members have the right to form 'tendencies' when this contributes to the free expression of opinion and to intra-party pluralism and debate. Internal party referenda are envisaged for major issues and have regularly been held to establish the order in which candidates for the European Parliament are placed on the party list. Elected regional committees have a decisive say on the list of candidates that will run in each constituency; local branches are also entirely sovereign to decide on candidates to local elections except in large cities and regions where decisions are made by the CPC. The party's president is elected by Congress (SYN 2005).

While SYN can indeed be considered an internally democratic party that invites members' participation, the operation of institutionalised factions in many cases distorts the members' voice, while many of the above-mentioned participative procedures have often become the locus of factional friction (Eleftheriou 2009; Tsakatika 2009; Vernardakis 2011, pp. 290–292). Moreover, low levels of participation in party procedures and the relative financial weakness of many local branches (a broad network of which was inherited largely by the KKE-es and EAR when SYN was set up) in practice do much to centralise party decision-making procedures. By the end of the 1990s, a considerable proportion of its members were disappointed by what they saw as the party's factionalism and excessive introspection and the party's membership was in decline.[5]

SYN's organisational response both to the primary aim of appealing to younger cohorts and to its own members' grievances about the internal functioning of the party came in 2001. It involved establishing a political and electoral alliance with a host of smaller parties, groups and networks of the extra-parliamentary left in the context of the Συνασπισμός της Ριζοσπαστικής Αριστεράς (Coalition of the Radical Left [SYRIZA]),[6] which offered the party an open, pluralist, unitary and more radical profile. SYN was and remained (until 2012) the largest party in the SYRIZA coalition, representing at least 80 per cent of its cadres, activists and voters. SYRIZA was one of the core choices of the party's new leadership after 2000 and was promoted as part and parcel of the party's 'left turn', much to the dismay of the minority faction (Eleftheriou 2009). Setting up the SYRIZA coalition raised expectations that local party branches would open up to activists and non-members who are nonetheless 'active citizens' and that this would renew inter-party democracy and boost participation, particularly in the period between 2004 and 2008 under the leadership of Alekos Alavanos. However, these expectations were not fulfilled, mostly because SYRIZA by and large remained an alliance at the leadership level and did not evolve into a political unit with greater political cohesion or proceed to a merging of organisations at the local level. Nonetheless, through SYRIZA the party did to some extent succeed in modifying its social representation and in halting membership decline. While membership by and large remained stable over the last decade at over 16,000, the make-up of party members has changed slightly: fewer members from higher-income educated strata (fewer in rich neighbourhoods, more in the countryside) and more people whose first party membership was of SYN rather than of the KKE or the KKE-es (approaching 50 per cent in the 2010 congress); younger new members who are from SYN Youth but also from elsewhere (interview no. 1).

SYN's approach to environmental linkage is heavily influenced by the tradition of the Italian left, which highlights the principles of mutuality and autonomy. For SYN, the role of the political left is 'not to guide but to participate in movements and try to influence them, while learning from them' (interview no. 5). Consistent with its attempt to reach out particularly to the younger cohorts, the most evident recent development in terms of SYN's links to civil society organisations has been its effort to establish contacts with the new social movements that emerged over the decade and were mostly associated with younger generations of activists. Νεολαία Συνασπισμού (SYN Youth), the party's youth organisation, has been the key intermediary between the party and the social movements; its members range in age from 16 to 28 years. Until 2012 SYN Youth numbered about 1,500 members, most of whom were university students (interview no. 6). SYN Youth's foundation and consolidation (1999–2006) was coterminous with its engagement with the anti-globalisation movement, which meant that its identity and core policy agenda (social rights, anti-hierarchy, anti-capitalism, radical ecology, feminism, an international as opposed to a European horizon of struggle) were deeply influenced by it. It was mainly SYN Youth cadres that were the motivating force behind the formation of the Ελληνικό Κοινωνικό Φόρουμ (Greek Social Forum [EKF]) and the 20-member coordinating committee of the 4th European Social Forum (ESF) that took place in Athens in 2006. SYN Youth's strong presence in the 4th ESF was partly due to the fact that the event was supported economically and logistically with resources that SYN's trade unionists managed to squeeze out of GSEE (interviews nos 2 and 3). It can also be partly explained by the fact that the KKE had decided not to join the EKF. SYN Youth has also been visibly involved in the anti-war movement (2003), the movement of solidarity towards immigrants, the university students' movement (2006, 2007) and, more controversially, the anti-authoritarian movement that emerged after the police shooting of 15-year-old Alexis Grigoropoulos in Athens in December 2008.

While SYN's newly leading faction was initially hesitant, in due course it encouraged and particularly after 2004 actively supported its youth wing's engagement with social movements. This was due to the fact that young SYN cadres and young people more generally (SYN's core target group) were not inclined to become active in Greek trade unions, as they perceived them as too bureaucratic and dominated by mainstream political forces, whereas the prospect of participation in social movements seemed to be more palatable (interview no. 2). SYN Youth drew in numerous new recruits from among the young activists of the new social movements, building up its cadre pool and preparing them for leadership roles in the party. Furthermore, a new microcosm was created around SYN Youth which helped integrate not only young recruits but also new members and sympathisers of SYN. The festival of SYN Youth and its summer camp, to provide two examples, became popular annual meeting places for 'the people of the left'. Through leadership overlap and cooptation (Schwartz 2005) among leading social movement activists, as well as through the creation of a new microcosm to integrate them, SYN and its youth organisation were thus highly successful in their aims when it came to cultivating links to social movements.

SYN also attempted to reorganise and strengthen its links to trade unions, but with limited results. Its activity unfolded at two levels: first, at confederation level, the group Αυτόνομη Παρέμβαση (Autonomous Intervention [AI]) was founded in 2002 with the purpose of being the face of the trade unionists close to the party in the elected executive boards of both major trade union confederations. Its greatest strength is in the public sector, particularly among education and health professionals and in the professional associations of lawyers, engineers, etc., while in the private sector its support is mainly in the former state utilities (now mostly privatised). The formation of AI did not augment the party's influence in the trade union movement, although that influence remained stable over the decade.[7] Formally AI is independent from SYN but in practice it is closely linked to the party through membership and cadre overlap. Informal coordination takes places through the Department of Labour policy of the party's CPC, in which the leading cadres of AI participate. Autonomous Intervention makes its own decisions but within the parameters of SYN/SYRIZA positions (interview no. 3).

Second, the Δίκτυο Συνδικαλιστών ΣΥΡΙΖΑ (SYRIZA Network of Trade Unionists) was assembled in 2007, the purpose of which was to contribute to the horizontal coordination of new trade unions, active at the first level of the trade union pyramid (Tsakiris 2010). In contrast to PAME's sectarian logic, the network's aim was not 'to substitute, but to complement' action at the level of trade union confederations (interviews nos 2 and 3). New trade unions, which in some instances do not participate in one of the GSEE's federations or centres, cover workers in publishing, telecoms, computers, courier services, translation and new banking services, members aged under 35 years being their backbone (interview no. 3). The SYRIZA network, however, did not succeed in bringing the party any considerable gains in terms of recruiting cadres or increasing its political influence in the new unions.

SYN's internal democratic operation and openness to new members, activists and supporters as well as its pluralist and unitary appeal to social movements and organisations of civil society were successful only in part over the last decade, particularly with regard the new ties it built with younger cohorts and social movements but less so with groups of precarious private sector workers and the trade union movement. Pluralism was a double-edged sword: SYN was internally plagued by political division and factional strife throughout most of the last decade, a state of affairs that in turn limited its potential appeal to a broader range of disaffected citizens, members and civil society groups.

The Greek Radical Left in the Economic Crisis

The 2008 financial crisis marked the beginning of a new era for Greek politics. Not long after 2009, when PASOK defeated the ruling ND in a landslide election, the global financial crisis reached Greece, giving rise to a dramatic sovereign debt crisis. The country's government resorted to 'bailout' packages provided by the European Union and the International Monetary Fund (IMF) on condition they implemented unprecedented fiscal austerity measures, rapid structural reforms and extensive privatisation of state resources. The policies introduced led to severe recession and a rise in unemployment levels, and the sovereign debt crisis was quickly transformed into an economic crisis, which in turn triggered a full-scale political crisis.

Levels of social mobilisation had been on the rise since 2009, with tens of thousands participating in street demonstrations against government austerity policies, the emergence of new social movements, and general strikes called by the trade unions (Kouvelakis 2011). The post-1974 two-party system was already heavily threatened by the rising tide of anti-party sentiment, which reflected generalised perceptions of the incompetence of the mainstream parties (the centre-left PASOK and the centre-right ND) (Constantinidis & Tsakatika 2011), defections of leading MPs from their ranks and increasing levels of social protest; after three years of political instability, the system collapsed in the dual elections of May and June 2012. New Democracy's strength was halved and PASOK's vote share diminished by 75 per cent. Three new political actors emerged, each winning around seven per cent of the vote, namely the party of the Δημοκρατική Αριστερά (Democratic Left, DIMAR), a recent split from SYN, Ανεξάρτητοι Έλληνες (Independent Greeks), a recent split from ND, and the extreme-right Χρυσή Αυγή (Golden Dawn).

Another equally important development was the major shift that took place in the electoral geography of the radical left. Both SYN and the KKE had over the last decade followed a consistent protest strategy which opposed government policies and prioritised linkage to their members, trade unions and social movements; they had also taken a clear-cut policy position against the austerity measures and supported the strikes and social mobilisation that emerged with all their available political and organisational resources. As a result, they were less subject to the legitimacy crisis that hit the party system in 2012 and found themselves in a stronger position with respect to their mainstream competitors. SYN/SYRIZA nevertheless was the party that benefited spectacularly from the two electoral battles and managed to overtake KKE in vote share for the first time in their common history (Table 1). While SYRIZA nearly quadrupled its vote share (see Table 1), hijacking the PASOK vote particularly among less privileged, unemployed and younger groups (Vernardakis 2012), the KKE's share of the vote was halved, with grave losses to SYRIZA. A new coalition government was formed by ND, PASOK and DIMAR in June 2012, SYRIZA becoming the country's second-largest political force and taking on the main opposition role after transforming itself into a unified party. While the two radical left parties' different approaches to linkage highlight only one of the factors that contributed to SYRIZA's rise and the KKE's downfall, it is clear that SYRIZA's linkage strategy was more successful over the crisis period. In the remainder of this section we will try to identify the main reasons.

After 2010, internal pluralism stopped being a weakness for SYN and SYRIZA, turning into a clear advantage. The exit of the 'Renewal Wing' faction from SYN (which evolved into DIMAR) in the summer of 2010 curtailed political disagreement and factional infighting within SYN and resulted in the effective dominance of Alexis Tsipras's leadership in both SYN and SYRIZA. In turn, this development (together with certain facets of Greek electoral law that favour parties over coalitions of parties) facilitated the decision to transform SYRIZA into a unified party on the eve of the June 2012 elections. The process of organisational refoundation is currently underway. SYRIZA's coalitional structure, internal pluralism and openness, as well as the fact that it was itself a work in progress, provided an organisational locus that could easily include new groups, movements, activists and individual supporters that approached the coalition before and after the 2012 elections, mostly after abandoning PASOK. In that sense, SYRIZA's participatory linkage made it easier for the party to adapt to rapid electoral change. In contrast, KKE's centralised structure, strict membership policy, further organisational consolidation along sectoral/professional lines and the streamlining of all its other ancillary organisations (KNE 2010, pp. 19–24; interviews nos 4 and 7) to mirror PAME and suit its needs (Eleftheriou 2011) rendered the party more rigid and sectarian and made adaptation to the new situation difficult. KKE's participatory linkage strategy seemed to be relatively successful while voter preferences were relatively stable but proved ineffective at times of deep social change.

The greatest challenge for both parties' environmental linkage strategy was the emergence of new confrontational forms of social protest, such as 'Won't Pay', a movement of civil disobedience by citizens who refused to pay tolls on many of the country's highways (Tsakiris & Aranitou 2012) and, more crucially, the Greek 'Indignants' movement. The Indignants started out in May 2011 as an anti-party and anti-political protest movement that occupied central squares in Athens and other major Greek cities (Georgiadou, Kafe & Pierides 2012) but was soon transformed into a hothouse for the ideas of both the radical left and the nationalist right. In practice the Indignants contested KKE's dominance of social mobilisation through PAME, and invited harsh criticism of the party. According to the KKE, the Indignants' protests were instigated by SYRIZA, the extra-parliamentary left and nationalists who 'chose to conceal their political identity and exploit the demonstrators' anger' (interview no. 9). Only the protests called by PAME were conducted according to appropriate organisational principles and were endowed with a genuine anti-systemic political orientation. These were features that the Indignants' movement lacked, according to the KKE (Gogos 2011). This was a familiar line of argument that the KKE had adopted against most social movements, including the global justice movement, over the decade. In contrast to the KKE, SYN was positively supportive of the 'Won't Pay!' movement (Tsakiris & Aranitou 2012), while some of SYN's cadres also played an active role in the Indignants movement. Economists and intellectuals close to the party as well as members of SYN Youth participated and on occasion played a leading role in the general assembly and the panel discussions that were organised in Athens's Syntagma Square. The Indignants were not, however, a product of SYRIZA's steering: they were initially organised through social networking sites by mostly young, progressive and educated non-partisans (interview no. 8). SYN stood as an informal advocate of the movement in the political sphere and offered a political narrative that explained and justified the movement's emergence. In that sense, it largely succeeded in being identified with the Indignants movement regardless of its actual contribution to the latter's onset.

At the level of trade unions, PAME called and organised its own strikes at national, sectoral and local level. A very successful example of a local strike was the 264-day strike at the Aspropyrgos Steel Industry, which mobilised local KKE support committees ('Popular Committees') throughout the neighbouring cities and several PAME-affiliated trade unions. On certain occasions, national PAME strikes were planned for the same days as the general strikes called by GSEE and Ανώτατη Διοίκηση Ενώσεων Δημοσίων Υπαλλήλων (Confederation of Greek Civil Servants' Trade Unions, ADEDY). However, the demonstrations that PAME called were deliberately separate from those called by the other trade unions. In contrast, SYN, AI and the SYRIZA network of trade unionists actively supported the general strikes called by GSEE and ADEDY. SYN's influence in trade unions was limited until 2012 and therefore this was not an area where it could make its presence strongly felt between 2008 and 2012. The crisis initially challenged SYN and SYRIZA by exposing their weakness in the labour movement, but their unitary appeal for a cohesive and combative trade union movement was successful in that it made it easier for former PASOK-affiliated trade unionists to approach SYRIZA after the 2012 elections.

All things considered, SYRIZA's political support of social movements and inclusive discourse gave the impression of a coalition eager to cooperate with and unite a broad range of social and political forces. On the contrary, the KKE's vanguardism and refusal to cooperate with other forces of the left, including SYRIZA, cost it dearly in terms of its appeal to a broader electorate as well as to its own voters and members. It seems that SYRIZA capitalised on its pro-movement stance, while the KKE was punished for its sectarian stance by the very strata that were the focus of its political appeals.

Conclusions

Principally in response to the fact that their social legitimacy had been considerably weakened in the early 1990s, KKE and SYN turned to an old but neglected friend from the late 1990s onwards: civil society. All things considered, their decade-long efforts up to 2012 can be deemed successful in electoral terms. Electoral results can certainly not be directly and fully attributed to the parties' linkage strategies, nor do they accurately reflect the perception of their social legitimacy among the electorate. Nonetheless, both parties had ensured their parliamentary representation and stabilised their share of the vote; they even made modest gains in the national elections, particularly after 2007 (Table 1). More importantly, they were successful in strengthening their participatory and environmental linkages in terms of stabilising their membership, creating 'microcosms', or subcultures through which they socialised and integrated their members and sympathizers, and forging new ties to, respectively, the labour movement (KKE) and the new social movements (SYN).

Legacy plays a significant part in explaining the difference in the way the two parties of the left went about pursuing linkage and the implications for their own organisational and programmatic development. Both parties' ideological origins and organisational models predisposed them to make specific choices about the type of linkage they could pursue and with whom, which in turn fed back into those templates, reinforcing them, following a 'path-dependent' logic (Hall & Taylor 1996). Those entrenched linkage strategies were put to the test by external events. While the KKE's approach to linkage counter-intuitively seemed to be more successful over the best part of the decade, SYRIZA's approach which emphasised pluralism and openness to social movements proved more adept in the fluid political environment of the 2008–12 period. It seems that the economic crisis has radically altered the Greek party system, presenting SYN/SYRIZA and KKE with roles that are very different from those they were accustomed to. Whether their 'turn towards civil society' will survive electoral defeat in the case of the KKE, and government-in-waiting status in the case of SYRIZA, remains to be seen.

Acknowledgements

The authors would like to thank Giorgos Bithimitris for his assistance with preliminary research, and André Freire, Manos Matsaganis, two anonymous referees and the editors of *South European Society and Politics* for their comments. Myrto Tsakatika would like to acknowledge financial assistance generously offered by the Carnegie Trust for the Universities of Scotland for completing parts of this research.

Notes

[1] Union density in Greece is estimated to have dropped from 34 per cent in 1990 to 24 per cent in 2008 (Organisation for Economic Cooperation and Development [OECD] 2011).

[2] GSEE represents private sector employees as well as workers from sectors formerly in the broader public sector, such as telecommunications, energy and banks, which make up the bulk of its membership. It consists of trade union federations—organised on a sectoral basis—and labour centres—organised on a territorial basis. Federations and labour centres consist of first-level unions. In political terms GSEE—much like ADEDY, the other main Greek trade union confederation—was dominated until 2012 by trade unionists affiliated primarily to the centre-left PASOK and in second place to the centre-right ND.

[3] PAME's strength in GSEE has been extremely stable over the years, at about 21 per cent.

[4] Influence in the students' unions varied between five and ten per cent until 1996 and since 2000 the figure has stabilised above 15 per cent.

[5] SYN had 22,971 members when the party was established in 1992 and then gradually declined to 16,376 in 2004 (Eleftheriou 2009). In June 2010 a minor party split led to about 3000 members leaving the party to form DIMAR (interview no. 1).

[6] The components of SYRIZA—apart from SYN—in 2012 were as follows: the Trotskyist groups Κόκκινο (Red), Διεθνιστική Εργατική Αριστερά (Internationalist Workers' Left, DEA) and Ξεκίνημα (Beginning); the Maoist group Κομμουνιστική Οργάνωση Ελλάδας (Communist Organisation of Greece, KOE); the KKE dissidents' Κίνηση για την Ενότητα Δράσης της Αριστεράς (Movement for the Unity of Action of the Left, KEDA); the left social-democratic party Δημοκρατικό Κοινωνικό Κίνημα, DIKKI); Manolis Glezos's (a prominent figure of the Greek Resistance) Ενεργοί Πολίτες (Active Citizens); the Οικοσοσιαλιστές Ελλάδας (Ecosocialists of Greece); the political group of PASOK dissidents Νέος Αγωνιστής (New Fighter); the small left groups Ομάδα Ρόζα (Rosa Group), Ριζοσπάστες (Radicals) and Αντικαπιταλιστική Πολιτική Ομάδα (Anticapitalist Political Group, APO).

[7] AI has steadily commanded about six per cent in GSEE and eight per cent in ADEDY.

References

Allern, E. H. & Bale, T. (2012) 'Political parties and interest groups: disentangling complex relationships', *Party Politics*, vol. 18, no. 1, pp. 7–25.

Bale, T. & Dunphy, R. (2011) 'In from the cold? Left parties and government involvement since 1989', *Comparative European Politics*, vol. 9, no. 3, pp. 269–291.

Bithimitris, G. (2008) 'Στρατηγικές του συνδικαλιστικού κινήματος: η συγκρουσιακή διάσταση – η περίπτωση του ΠΑΜΕ' [Trade union strategies: the contentious dimension – the case of PAME], mimeo, Athens.

Clogg, R. (1987) *Parties and Elections in Greece. The Search for Legitimacy*, Duke University Press, Durham, NC.

Constantinidis, G. & Tsakatika, M. (2011) '"Αντιδικομματισμός" και αντικομματικά συναισθήματα στην Ελλάδα' ['Anti-bipartyism' and anti-party sentiments in Greece], in *Η κοινή γνώμη στην Ελλάδα (2008–2010)* [Public Opinion in Greece (2008–2010)], ed. C. Vernardakis, Savalas, Athens, pp. 65–100.

Dalton, R. & Wattenberg, M. (eds) (2000) *Parties without Partisans. Political Change in Advanced Industrial Democracies*, Oxford University Press, Oxford.

Doukas, G. (1991) 'The thirteenth congress of the KKE: defeat of the renovators', *Journal of Communist Studies*, vol. 7, no. 3, pp. 393–398.

Eleftheriou, C. (2009) 'The "uneasy symbiosis". Factionalism and radical politics in Synaspismos', paper presented at the 4th PhD Symposium of the LSE Hellenic Observatory, London, 25–26 June.

Eleftheriou, C. (2011) 'Κομματική στρατηγική, οργανωτική αλλαγή και εκλογική κινητοποίηση: το KKE στις αυτοδιοικητικές εκλογές του 2010' (Party strategy, organisational change and electoral mobilisation: the KKE at the 2010 local elections], *Greek Political Science Review*, no. 37, pp. 69–97.

Eleftheriou, C. (forthcoming) 'Το "παλίμψηστο" της ριζοσπαστικής αριστεράς κατά την περίοδο 1991–2009. KKE και Συνασπισμός υπό τη "σκιά" του κράτους' [The 'palimpsest' of radical left during the period 1991–2009. KKE and Synaspismos under the 'shadow' of the state], in *Κρίσεις και Μετασχηματισμοί στον Ελληνικό Κοινωνικό Σχηματισμό* [Crises and Transformations in the Greek Social Formation], ed. M. Spourdalakis, Savalas, Athens.

Georgiadou, V., Kafe, A. & Pierides, C. (2012) 'Anti-party, anti-parliamentary or anti-democratic social movements of the "Outraged" citizens in Greece', paper presented at the 22nd World Congress of the International Political Science Association, Madrid, 8–12 July.

Gogos, T. (2011) 'Οι εργάτες μπορούν να σταματήσουν κάθε μηχανισμό υπονόμευσης' [The workers can stop any mechanism of subversion], *Ριζοσπάστης* [The Radical], 5 July.

Hall, P. & Taylor, R. C. R. (1996) 'Political science and the three new institutionalisms', *Political Studies*, vol. 44, no. 5, pp. 936–957.

Kalyvas, S. & Marantzidis, N. (2002) 'Greek communism, 1968–2001', *East European Politics and Societies*, vol. 16, no. 3, pp. 665–690.

Kapetanyannis, B. (1979) 'The making of Greek Eurocommunism', *Political Quarterly*, vol. 50, no. 4, pp. 445–460.

Kapetanyannis, B. (1993) 'The left in the 1980s: too little, too late', in *Greece 1981–1989. The Populist Decade*, ed. Richard Clogg, Macmillan Press, London, pp. 78–93.

Katz, R. S. & Mair, P. (1995) 'Changing models of party organization and party democracy: the emergence of the cartel party', *Party Politics*, vol. 1, no. 1, pp. 5–28.

Kitschelt, H. (1988) 'Left-libertarian parties: explaining innovation in competitive party systems', *World Politics*, vol. 40, no. 2, pp. 194–234.

KKE (1996a) 'Programme of the KKE', available online at: inter.kke.gr/Documents/docprogr/

KKE (1996b) 'Statutes of the KKE', available online at: inter.kke.gr/Documents/docstatutes/

KKE (2005) '17th Congress political resolution', available online at: inter.kke.gr/Documents/17cong/polit-resolut-17thcong/

KNE (2010) *10ο Συνέδριο. Απόφαση* [10th Congress. Resolution], Athens.

Kouvelakis, S. (2011) 'The Greek cauldron', *New Left Review*, vol. 72, pp. 17–32.

Kretsos, L. (2011) 'Union responses to the rise of precarious youth employment in Greece', *Industrial Relations Journal*, vol. 42, no. 5, pp. 453–472.

Lawson, K. (ed.) (1980) *Political Parties and Linkage: A Comparative Perspective*, Yale University Press, New Haven.

Matsaganis, M. (2007) 'Union structures and pension outcomes in Greece', *British Journal of Industrial Relations*, vol. 45, no. 3, pp. 537–555.

March, L. (2011) *Radical Left Parties in Europe*, Routledge, London.

OECD (2011) 'OECD.StatExtracts: trade union density', available online at: http://stats.oecd.org/Index.aspx?DataSetCode=UN_DEN# (accessed 29 August 2012).

PAME (1999) 'Constitution', available online at: pamehellas.gr/content_fullstory.php?pg=1&s=1&lang=2

Pridham, G. & Verney, S. (1991) 'The coalitions of 1989–90 in Greece: inter-party relations and democratic consolidation', *West European Politics*, vol. 14, no. 4, pp. 42–69.

Schwartz, M. (2005) 'Linkage processes in party networks', in *Political Parties and Political Systems: the Concept of Linkage Revisited*, eds A. Römmele, D. Farrell & P. Ignazi, Praeger, Westport, CT, pp. 37–60.

SYN (1992) 'Η Πολιτική Απόφαση του 1ου Συνεδρίου του Συνασπισμού' [The Political resolution of Synaspismos 1st Congress], available online at: http://www.syn.gr/gr/keimeno.php?id=13386

SYN (2003) 'Προγραμματικές Κατευθύνσεις' [Programmatic directions], available online at: http://www.syn.gr/downloads/program2003.pdf

SYN (2005) 'Καταστατικό του Συνασπισμού της Αριστεράς, των Κινημάτων και της Οικολογίας' [Statutes of Synaspismos], available online at: http://www.syn.gr/downloads/syn_katastatiko.pdf

Tsakatika, M. (2009) 'Από το "κριτικό ναι" στο φιλοευρωπαϊκό "όχι". Τι έχει αλλάξει στον Ευρωπαϊκό προσανατολισμό του Συνασπισμού;' [The Greek Coalition of the Left: turning Eurosceptic?], *International and European Politics*, vol. 13–14, pp. 143–161.

Tsakiris, A. (2010) 'The Greek December 2008 uprising and the role of the new trade unions', paper presented at the 15th Alternative Futures and Popular Protest Conference, Manchester, 29–31 March.

Tsakiris, A. & Aranitou, V. (2012) '"Under the weight of the social": reactions of the social representation system and anti-systemic challenges during the era of the Memorandum', paper presented at the 22nd World Congress of the International Political Science Association, Madrid, 8–12 July.

Vernardakis, C. (2011) *Πολιτικά κόμματα, εκλογές και κομματικό σύστημα. Οι μετασχημα ετασχηματισμοί της πολιτικής αντιπροσώπευσης εϑϑι διει [Political Parties, Elections and Party System. The Transformations of Political Representation 1990–2010], Sakkoulas, Athens.*

Vernardakis, C. (2012) 'Οι εκλογές της 17ης Ιουνίου και οι νέες τομές στο κομματικό σύστημα' [The June 17th elections and the new cleavages in the Greek party system], *Αυγή* [Dawn], 24 June.

Verney, S. (1989) '"Compromesso storico": reunion and renewal on the Greek left', *Journal of Communist Studies*, vol. 5, no. 4, pp. 200–206.

Interviews

Interview 1	Secretary of SYN's Central Political Committee, Athens, 5 April 2011.
Interview 2	Member of SYN's Political Secretariat, former secretary of AI, Athens, 6 April 2011.
Interview 3	Member of SYN's Political Secretariat, Central Political Committee Department of Labour Policy, Athens, 6 April 2011.
Interview 4	President of the Federation of Greek Women (OGE), Athens, 7 April 2011.
Interview 5	Member of SYN's Political Secretariat, former secretary of SYN Youth, leading activist in Greek Social Forum, Athens, 7 April 2011.
Interview 6	Secretary of SYN Youth, Athens, 2 June 2011.
Interview 7	Member of Students' Militant Front (MAS) executive secretariat, member of KNE central council, Athens, 6 June 2011.
Interview 8	Social activist, journalist, SYN' s consultant on social media, Skype interview, 14 November 2011.
Interview 9	Member of PAME's Youth Secretariat, member of KKE's Central Committee Trade Union Department, Athens, 23 December 2011.

Myrto Tsakatika (PhD Essex) is a Lecturer in Politics at the School of Social and Political Sciences, University of Glasgow. Her research interests lie in European Union and South European politics. Her latest publications have appeared in international peer-reviewed journals such as the *Journal of Common Market Studies*, *Journal of European Public Policy* and *Europe–Asia Studies*.

Costas Eleftheriou is a PhD candidate at the University of Athens. His main interests include: Greek party politics, European radical left parties, and philosophy of political science. In his PhD thesis he examines the KKE's organisational and ideological development during the last two decades. He currently works as a political analyst at the National Confederation of Hellenic Commerce.

A Society within Society: Linkage in the Case of the Cypriot Communist Party

Giorgos Charalambous and Christophoros Christophorou

In this article we aim to contribute to the study of linkage by focusing on the Cypriot communist party—Progressive Party of the Working People (AKEL), an exceptional case in European communism—between the mid-1980s and the present. Based on the distinction between participatory and environmental linkage, we explore three issues. First, we focus on the intensity of linkage processes through the examination of participation patterns and organisational practices in the party. Then, we trace the predominant direction of influence between AKEL and society. Finally, we assess the explanatory value of four potential factors—ideology, electoral competition, party leadership and party model—on the links developed by AKEL with society.

Within the cosmos of West European communism, and more broadly the European radical left, Ανορθωτικό Κόμμα Εργαζομένου Λαού (Progressive Party of the Working People, AKEL) is an exceptional case. It is significant because of its electoral fortune, especially after the events of 1989–91 (Charalambous 2007; Christophorou 2006). In the 2001 parliamentary election the party reached 34.7 per cent, and since then it has enduringly maintained an electoral appeal above 30 per cent. More recently, AKEL General Secretary Dimitris Christofias won the 2008 presidential election and was elected to office, making AKEL the first radical left party in the European Union (EU) to become the main party of government.

The only instance when the party polled 'badly' was in 1985, when an alignment with its traditional opponent, the right-wing Δημοκρατικός Συναγερμός (Democratic Rally, DISY) against the centrist President's handling of the Cyprus Problem, ended in a loss of approximately five percentage points. This was also the beginning of an internal battle between the 'reformers' and the 'orthodox' leadership. In early 1990 the reformers either left or were expelled from their leadership positions and from the party. Joined by other forces, they formed a new party, the Ανανεωτικό Δημοκρατικό Σοσιαλιστικό Κίνημα (Democratic Socialist Renewal Movement, ADISOK). This new party initially failed to enter parliament and then merged, in 1996, with the liberals to form Ενωμένοι Δημοκράτες (United Democrats, EDI), today a very small movement.

AKEL also stands out because of its successful employment of a mass model of party organisation, which is no longer a defining characteristic of most European radical left parties (Bale & Dunphy 2007; see also Charalambous 2012). It exhibits mass membership and mass ancillary organisations (we explore this issue later). It is structured on the basis of an extensive and articulate membership organisation of branches and cells, run by professionals or semi-professionals. It enforces party discipline through the application of democratic centralism (Krouwel 2006, as cited in Charalambous 2012, p. 243)[1]. Along with the virtual absence of factions, or even clear lines of division within its ranks in the post-1990 period, the above characteristics render AKEL a very cohesive organisation with great mobilisation potential.

Thus, AKEL diverges from observed patterns across the European radical left in at least two respects: electoral and organisational. Overall, it does not fit the conditions taken as starting points by the dominant theories and accounts of communist and radical left party adaptation (see Botella & Ramiro 2003).[2] Neither does its experience to date fit the claim that socio-economic and other developments have rendered the mass model of party organisation inadequate for contemporary electoral competition (Katz & Mair 1995). With these features as our background, we aim to give an account of how and why AKEL has tailored its participatory and environmental linkages with society during the past 25 years. It is important to stress, nevertheless, that AKEL has shared the experience of internal crisis and electoral setback with the rest of the European radical left, albeit for a brief period of time. Starting our empirical analysis from the mid-1980s, when the party experienced substantial vote losses and a five-year spell of internal upheaval, our more specific purpose is to juxtapose its difficult years (those which make it more similar to its counterparts in Europe) with its more trouble-free ones.

First, through the examination of participation patterns and organisational practices, we interrogate the intensity of linkage processes. Membership size and levels of participation as well as their evolution can help us draw a picture of the quantitative aspect of the participatory linkage. The quantitative aspect, however, can either be accompanied by the more qualitative aspect of strong membership rights, or not. The main membership rights concern candidate and leadership selection as well as the decision-making process for party policies. Such rights may be granted strategically and in response to internal or external dynamics (Le Duc 2001; Scarrow, Webb & Farrell 2000).

Second, regarding environmental linkage, we consider the diversity (or diversification) of the party's links with civil society organisations (CSOs) and the extent of connection between parties and CSOs (Allern 2010). Does the party target a wide constituency of societal voices? How institutionalised or embedded are the party's links with each of these voices? The direction of influence between the party and CSOs can signal organisational change or its absence. According to Poguntke, 'votes are exchanged for policies, or more realistically, policy pledges' (Poguntke 2006, p. 396). Particularly in the case of parties that experience electoral decline or stagnation, there is increased likelihood of programmatic transfer from CSOs to parties (policies being adopted by parties at the request of CSOs and in exchange for votes) and organisational restructuring on behalf of parties (so that they can become more receptive to the policy requests of CSOs). Concurrently, there is decreased likelihood of influence by parties on CSOs. AKEL's status as an established mass, and electorally successful, organisation reverses the hypothesis. We are led to expect that programmatic transfer from CSOs towards the party, and organisational restructuring inside the party will be less likely than any tangible influence of AKEL on CSOs. If, at the time when others experience electoral decline, AKEL continues to be strong, then it may be able to influence CSOs and have limited motives to adjust its structures and policies so as to accommodate their demands.

Third, we assess the explanatory value of four potential factors on the links developed by AKEL with society. What follows is not an exhaustive list, as existing studies have advanced a number of explanations, either internal to the parties themselves, or affecting parties' overall 'incentive structures' (Allern & Bale 2012). Our selection of factors reflects the purpose of approaching AKEL within the contours of its own distinctive status.

First of all, as a communist party, in contrast to other non-communist radical left parties, AKEL's links to civil society are strongly influenced by its ideology (Backes & Moreau 2008). In so far as communist ideology is different from other radical left ideologies (e.g. new left, democratic socialist, red-green, etc.), the party will most probably be inspired by communist interpretations of the significance, value and type of CSOs that it will seek association with, as well as by the organisational structures and procedures of the archetypal communist party.

Second, as an electorally successful communist party, AKEL's linkage is strongly affected by the dynamics of electoral competition. An opening up to CSOs, new members and more decentralised internal processes is more likely following an electoral loss or setback (in the case of AKEL, the electoral result of the 1985 elections) and a challenge by newly formed parties (the ADISOK splinter).

Third, as a case with no observable factions or lines of division in the post-1990 period but an internal crisis immediately before then, AKEL's linkage to civil society is likely to be explained by reference to the party leadership. Either factional struggle or the need for a new leadership to establish itself may condition a party's environmental linkage (Panebianco 1988, p. 191; see also Hopkin 2001, p. 4).

Fourth, as party of the mass type, the links AKEL establishes with civil society may be explained by reference to the party model. A mass party may be thought to be able to foster a strong relationship with trade unions (Allern 2010) but may also limit the incentive of the party leadership to link with other CSOs or to enlarge its membership.

Linkage in the Case of AKEL

Extent of Participatory Linkage: Party Membership and Participation

In contrast to other European parties, AKEL's membership has remained high and stable since the 1960s, with about 14,000 members (Christophorou 2006). The numerical strength at a time when left parties almost everywhere else in Europe have seen decreases in membership can be attributed, at least in part, to country-specific factors, such as clientelism, patronage and the power of family tradition. This is confirmed by the fact that high membership levels can also be observed in the right-wing DISY as well as other parties (Christophorou 2006; 2008, p. 93). Membership stability appears to be a deliberate choice that can be attributed, mostly, to AKEL's will to secure disciplined and efficient organisation while avoiding any sudden changes to its basic features (Ierodiakonou 2003). Stable membership figures also indicate the presence of a sustained demand.

According to the party statutes, membership requires approval by the majority of members of the party cell into which the applicant will be admitted. This decentralised process provides safer filtering and selection based on personal contact with applicants. Given the significant membership of AKEL's ancillary organisations (see later), it may be assumed that this pool constitutes the main, if not exclusive, source of members. The provision that the decision for admitting applicants coming from other political parties lies with the District Committee (DC), in the case of ordinary members, or with the Central Committee (CC), if the applicant be an official of another party, is indicative of the distinction made between what is labelled the 'Popular Movement' (or 'People's Movement') and other CSOs. More importantly, the caution exhibited towards those coming from outside the Popular Movement indicates the special care taken to avoid unwarranted influences.

Participation in the party at relatively high but stable levels, is not without problems. Official reports refer to persisting problems of productivity, participation in meetings, mobilisation and recruitment of cadres. Party cell meetings are often held three or four times a year instead of once a month and the members' average rate of participation, since 1990, has been below 50 per cent. The issues are 'fatigue, indifference, lack of discipline, tendencies to increase personal influence, and reduced contribution to the practical daily work of the party' (Christophorou 2006, pp. 521–522). These problems have been consistently reported by the CC and in congress resolutions, especially since 1990. They are mainly attributed to the values and culture of the capitalist society that promotes individualism as well as contempt for organised politics and political activism (AKEL 1990; 2006). But they also echo the clientelism-centred mentality in Cypriot society and the possibility that some of the non-active members joined the party because of family tradition rather than genuine interest.

Extent of Participatory Linkage: Membership Rights

Amendments to the party statute and rules of procedure by the party congress in 1990 provided for members to be part of the decision-making process on important policies. Since 1990 there have been various occasions on which members have been consulted: for example, on lifting the party's opposition to Cyprus's membership in the EU in 1995 (Christophorou 2006, pp. 519, 523) and on the proposal for AKEL's own candidacy (of Christofias) for the presidency of the Republic in 2007 (Charalambous 2009). Discussion revolved around the initial proposal of the CC (which was also the body that took the final decision that was then forwarded for approval to the congress) and was elaborated upon in various cell meetings by CC representatives. Unsurprisingly, the original decisions of the CC have never been changed or reversed, either before or at the congress.

Members' rights were also extended to procedures for nominating and electing delegates to party congresses and candidates to party governing bodies at various levels, including the CC. All the procedures now start at the party cell level. In 1990 secret voting was established in the elections for higher party organs. All members have the right to nominate and vote for the approval of the lists of delegates to the various assemblies. The lists are constituted according to quotas, based on party cell membership. Members also nominate and vote for candidates to the governing bodies at each level; they will then be approved by superior party organs, the candidates being ranked by special nominations committees.

Ranking criteria, which include commitment to the party, service, experience and other qualities, are a factor of leadership continuity and promotion. The vote to the party's governing bodies takes place at the party congress for the CC and the Central Control Committee (CCC), at the district congress for the DC, and so on. Similarly, the relevant body votes for its top officials—authority is collective and not individual, and the CC acts as the 'vanguard' of the party.

The election of the party congress is illustrative of the procedures followed since 1990 and of the powers exercised at various levels. Party cells elect their delegates to the congress and also nominate candidates to the CC and the CCC. Candidates to each of the two committees are presented on different ballots and delegates to the congress elect members by secret vote. However, the ranking of candidates by an 18-member nomination committee (NC) drawn from the Political Bureau (PB) or the CC (three) and the DCs (15), according to particular criteria, bestows significant discretionary powers upon that specific body but also on the PB, the CC and the DCs.

An additional matter is the extent to which the NC can deviate from the views and observations that the DCs forward to the CC, which also adds its own views and comments. The failed proposals to increase CC membership from 105 to 120 and replace ranking with an alphabetical order of candidates to the CC in the 2010 congress pointed to problems of distribution of powers and the impact that some practices may have on the functioning of the party. It seems that 90 per cent of the nomination committee's top candidates were elected in the CC despite the increased number of members who put themselves forward as candidates (264 candidates in 2010 against under 200 in the past) (Zorba 2010). The questions raised concern relations within the party, its members and officials and the quality of relations with civil society, in terms of the opportunities offered for contact and participation. If the distribution of influence and actual exercise of power within the party make it difficult for junior members to enter the hierarchy, how easy will it be for external individuals to participate and have their proposals heard or adopted?

Time of party membership requirements for the nomination of members as delegates—one year for secretaries of cells, two years for members of local/regional assemblies, three years for the district and the party congresses and seven years for the CC—make change an almost impossible mission. Moreover, within the context of these criteria, certain MPs and CC members or prospective CC members are promoted from the core central leadership (essentially those dealing with the party's daily affairs—the General Secretariat) at the expense of others. It is this leadership that ultimately conditions who will appear on TV, give a speech at a party conference or be appointed as head of one of the party's offices.

All the above points to a hierarchy built as a pyramid, with those standing in the upper levels having the power to assist selected people in the lower levels to get promoted. As in the strongly institutionalised ideal-type party described by Panebianco (1988, p. 60), careers can be made only by allowing oneself to be 'coopted by the centre'.

The more general picture of the party between 1990 and today illustrates the extensive initial renewal completed in the 18th congress of 1995 and the subsequent full consolidation of the new leadership. In the 1990 congress first-time participants (500) accounted for 39 per cent of the total (1401), while there were another 400 (32.7 per cent) new entrants in 1995, even though the number of delegates was reduced by almost 200. In spite of changes—university graduates (35.7 per cent) have replaced those with basic education, who declined from 40.8 per cent to 16.5 per cent—it clearly appears that the team put in place in 1990 and 1995 remains dominant. This is indicated by the low renewal rate of congress delegates—in 2000 (16.8 per cent), in 2005 (12.1 per cent) and in 2010 (12.7 per cent)—even though the overall number of delegates increased. Similarly, renewal in the CC was also limited as only 12 new members entered it in 2005 and less than 30 in 2010, following some voluntary departures or exclusions (AKEL 1990, 1996, 2001 and 2006; Zorba 2010). Consequently, there has been little change with respect to those holding power.

An additional field where members have gained more rights without significantly compromising centralisation is that of nominating candidates to elected public offices. This right was also extended to 'friends' of the party and made it possible for people outside the party's ancillary organisations to be nominated and run on AKEL's electoral tickets. Procedures for this selection raise a crucial issue: the extent of members' and friends' actual and effective powers. In the case of municipal and parliamentary elections, party members, cells, DCs and a number of special assemblies (of top party officials, members of governing bodies at all levels and representatives of the Popular Movement) all get involved in the shaping of the list of candidates that will be finalised by the CC. Such a decision-making process seems to involve broad consensus and participation. In practice, however, the fact that top-level officials take part in the selection process at lower levels offers them increased opportunities to influence the process from the start. Also, final decisions on the candidates' list incorporate a veto player function of the CC—which remains the controller of the final candidates' list—and a decisive role in the process for DCs.

In conclusion, the pyramidal structure of power, with the integration of lower bodies into a central bureaucracy, leaves little or no room for autonomous, decisive action by lower bodies, thus limiting attempts for bottom-up change (Kitschelt 1994, p. 212). It can be said that only in the case of local elections, at community level, do decisions lie with the local cells and the leaders of the local Popular Movement (women, youth, labour, farmers and the local club). Even there, though, control by the DC is possible.

Extent of Environmental Linkage: The Popular Movement

In order to illustrate the recent (non-)evolution of AKEL's links to CSOs we must delve into a historical period of Cypriot politics, the 1940s, that was very important for the left's development. In doing so, we are following Panebianco's (1988, p. xiii) argument that party organisations are largely constrained by their past and thus few of their aspects 'appear comprehensible if not traced to its [their] formative phase'.

AKEL was established in 1941 and eventually succeeded the Κομμουνιστικό Κόμμα Κύπρου (Communist Party of Cyprus, KKK), for which it acted as a front organisation until 1946. During the first ten years of its existence, it developed a very close relationship with a number of organisations that have acted as ancillary to the party itself. There are officially four such organisations:

1. Παγκύπρια Συντεχνιακή Επιτροπή (Pan-Cyprian Trade Unions' Committee, PSE) was formed in 1941 by various trade unions, which had been created in the 1930s, at a time when the party was organisationally weak but heavily involved in the unions. Inside AKEL, which was established a few months before PSE, the workers and the unions held the upper hand (Panayiotou 1999, ch. 5). Παγκύπρια Εργατική Ομοσπονδία (Pan-Cyprian Labour Federation, PEO) succeeded PSE in 1946.

2. Δημοκρατική Οργάνωση Νεολαίας (Progressive Organisation of Youth, AON) was established in 1944, and in 1959 it evolved into Ενιαία Δημοκρατική Οργάνωση Νεολαίας (Democratic Organisation of Youth, EDON). This organisation incorporates four sections: primary school children, high school pupils, university students and young professionals.

3. Ένωση Αγροτών Κύπρου (Cypriot Farmers' Union, EAK) was established in 1946 and was renamed Ένωση Κύπριων Αγροτών (Union of Cypriot Farmers, EKA) in 1959.

4. Παγκύπρια Οργάνωση Δημοκρατικών Γυναικών (Pan-Cyprian Organisation of Democratic Women, PODG) was established in 1950 and united the various progressive women's associations that arose in the 1940s. It became Παγκύπρια Ομοσπονδία Γυναικείων Οργανώσεων (Pan-Cyprian Federation of Women's Organisations, POGO) in 1959.

These ancillary organisations formed what came to be known as the Popular Movement. The historical conditions in which AKEL functioned[3] gave an impetus to the mass party model, as many interests and groups lacked representation in Cypriot society. Moreover, the Cypriot context is in contrast to countries where states financed parties from the beginning, offering them the opportunity to obtain their objectives from within political institutions (Van Biezen 1998, p. 32).

AKEL's links with PEO are organic in the sense that there is a significant degree of membership and leadership overlap between the two. All general secretaries of PEO since the 1940s have been members of AKEL's PB (with one early exception) and the number of PEO employees who are also members of the party has been approximately 95 per cent (interview, 25 July 2011, Nicosia). Trade union membership in the party is individual and not collective, as it has been in labour parties (Rawson 1969). Trade unionists can thus be more easily infused with a sense of loyalty to the party which surpasses the significance of their union affiliation. Something similar applies to EDON, POGO and EKA. Although all four of these organisations are formally autonomous, it has been the norm for members of AKEL's CC to occupy key positions in the main mass organisations, and for individuals active in the latter to move to key leadership positions in the party (Charalambous 2012, pp. 242–3). The more general picture is shown in Table 1, which presents data on the participation of AKEL CC members in the Popular Movement's organisations during the past 20 years. Since 1990 approximately one-quarter of the party CC has been composed of Popular Movement members, with leadership links to PEO being the strongest.

Table 1 Popular Movement Participation of AKEL CC Members* (%)

Popular Movement	2010	2005	2000	1995	1990
PEO	15	14	16	16	13
EDON	3	3	2	2	3
POGO	6	4	4	4	4
EKA	3	8	5	5	4
Total	27	29	27	27	24

*No such data exist for the composition of the party's CC before 1990.
Source: AKEL congresses (1990–2010). Figures have been rounded to whole numbers.

The growing number of members of AKEL's ancillary organisations vividly conveys the mass character of the party in the past 20 years. PEO had 60,556 members in 1980 and 81,453 in 2010, EDON's membership increased from 14,500 in 2001 to 19,400 in 2010, while EKA and POGO maintained membership levels in the area of 15,000 (Charalambous 2012, table 2). Yet, AKEL's societal presence has never exhausted itself in these four organisations. According to Panayiotou (1999, p. 451), by the 1940s the left's subculture had developed 'a triple organisational form with its core (the party) being "ideologically pure" (in a Leninist fashion), while the other two levels [one of them being the Popular Movement and the other being the aforementioned spheres of left activism] were increasingly more open to the general population'.

A prime example of the party's outer circle is Παγκύπρια Ένωση Μικροκαταστηματαρχών (Pan-Cyprian Union of Small Shopkeepers, PEM), established in 1942. In 1952 it evolved into Παγκύπριος Οργανισμός Βιοτεχνών και Επαγγελματιών Καταστηματαρχών (Pan-Cyprian Organisation of Artisans and Professional Shopkeepers, POVEK) to reflect a wider constituency. In 1997 it became a Federation and in 2006 a General Confederation, with more than 10,000 members and a very strong influence in its respective sector. It has traditionally supported AKEL's positions on economic issues and more recently those of the Christofias government.

Another trait of subculture is embodied in the educational associations (*μορφωτικοί σύλλογοι* or cultural clubs). These were established as lower-class ideological clubs in the 1920s and evolved into cultural associations in the 1940s, through the coordinated action of communist party activists. They were later transformed into institutions that emphasised sports and cultural activities (Panayiotou 1999, p. 456). The Football clubs Ομόνοια (Omonia) (based in Nicosia), Αλκή (Alki) and Σαλαμίνα (Salamina) (based in Larnaca) and ΑΕΛ (AEL, Αθλητική, Ένωση Λεμεσού, Athletic Union of Limassol) (based in Limassol) have also been traditionally associated with AKEL (Charalambous 2012, pp. 242–3). Members of AKEL's CC or other party bodies have occasionally served as presidents or board members of these clubs.

The significance of the above notwithstanding, AKEL's relations with society can only be fully seen when one examines the nature of the left–right cleavage and its impact on daily life. AKEL's almost unhindered development in the very early stages of its life, in 1941–42, fiercely opposed by an initially leaderless and non-organised conservative social body and the church, led to a deep, radical divide. The places where one sought to buy goods and services, the brands of coffee and other drinks and beverages one consumed, were dictated by the left–right cleavage and designated the camp one belonged to. AKEL promoted the creation of left-wing industries and businesses under the effective control of party officials and both camps mutually excluded their adversaries from employment (Peristianis 2006, p. 256).

While the impact of the cleavage may have weakened today, hundreds of families continue to earn their living in left-wing-controlled businesses that supply the market with products for daily consumption and services. The circular bond established between the party, employment, production and consumption reinforces AKEL's already strong influence on large parts of society.

The very strong cooperative movement and businesses in Cyprus (banks, supermarkets and product trading unions)[4] have also constituted a sector in which AKEL has extended its activity and influence since the 1940s. Linkage is enhanced through initiatives for the creation of mini societies and the presence of party cadres or even top officials in the governing bodies of cooperatives (including some of the big ones). This activity has many ramifications. There can be influence on decision-making, control of trade, financing of people, clubs and other organisations and the funding of entrepreneurial activities.

Extent of Environmental Linkage: Beyond the Popular Movement

In the renewal congress of 1990 (AKEL 1990, p. 106) the first reference was made to the duty of AKEL members to participate in mass organisations outside the Popular Movement—a dictum that was then repeated in every congress. Regular and close contacts and overlapping memberships exist with organisations active in fields important for AKEL's electoral and ideological profile, such as the resolution of the Cyprus Problem and the movement against racism and xenophobia.

With regard to the former field, the crucial link lies in the party's relations with the Παγκύπρια Ένωση Προσφύγων (Pan-Cyprian Union of Refugees, PEP). Consistent references have been made to PEP in AKEL's congresses since 1974, in addition to a substantial degree of membership overlap at the level of the two organisations' leading bodies. For instance, with the exception of a brief interlude, the president and other high officials of PEP have been members of the party's leading bodies (CC or PB). With regard to the second field mentioned above, the main example is in fact a non-governmental organisation (NGO), Κίνηση για Ισότητα, Στήριξη, Αντιρατσισμό (Movement for Equality, Support and Anti-racism, KISA), established in 1998 with the involvement of party members.

AKEL has, throughout its history, been involved in supporting the creation of CSOs. As an example, the first left-wing environmental movement—Περιβαλλοντική Κίνηση Κύπρου (Environmental Movement of Cyprus, PKK)—was founded through the involvement of people close to or inside the party. Since then PKK members have also been members of AKEL's various bodies and acted as candidates in parliamentary elections. The creation of PKK alerts us to AKEL's strategy of facing off emerging challenges. PKK was established in 1987, one year after the creation of the environmental movement Φίλοι του Ακάμα (Friends of Akamas), which coordinated its action with many established environmental and other types of organisations and, for the first time, brought ecological awareness and activism to the surface of Cyprus's social politics.

A look at the label of the party and its candidates' profiles is needed in order to fully grasp the 1990 changes' impact on the party's environmental linkage. While neither the description of AKEL as 'the party of the workers and the working people' nor the official name of the party has changed, both its electoral ticket and its political communication have been presented, since 1991, under the label 'AKEL–Left-New Forces'. This points to a party that has broadened both its features and its scope to embrace larger sections of society than those implied by the single label 'AKEL'. In addition to asserting the party's political coverage, the change could also act as an invitation to people beyond the traditional left-wing groups to join it.[5] Indeed, the loss of five per cent of the vote in the elections of 1985 was attributed, among other reasons, to the 'narrowness' of the party's ticket according to the report of the CC to the 1986 party congress, in which an additional selection criterion appeared—'functionality', meaning the inclusion of 'specialists that could offer their services in various sectors: economists, lawyers, doctors, engineers, educators and actors of cultural life'. This criterion and the inclusion of candidates of broader appeal were ignored, noted the report (AKEL 1986, p. 63).

It is interesting to consider the criteria for the constitution of the ticket for parliamentary elections, as laid out in the current rules of procedure: 'The ticket must be broad and representative, it must express the nature of the Party, of the Popular Movement and of the Left more generally. It must have an appropriate combination of Party members and Party friends, of various ages, men and women, and it must include political, social and other personalities' (AKEL 2011). The need to link with civil society, though without using this term, was expressed in the selection criteria, with the inclusion of 'political, social and other personalities', where the term 'personalities' is used in Greek to denote influential or authoritative persons.

No significant changes other than those of 1990 were implemented throughout the period examined. Only the CC's Theses to the 2010 congress went a step further. For the first time, a direct reference to the concept of NGOs was made. The Theses argued,

> Within but also outside the European Union there is a climate of encouragement for and support to the functioning of NGOs. The motives of this creation are not always pure, in the sense that evidently the ruling circles attempt to give NGOs a character and a content which counterbalances social and class struggle, partisan and syndicalist action. (AKEL 2010, p. 43)

The Theses, however, proceeded by noting that 'AKEL calls upon its members and the friends of the party to become active in non-governmental organisations and to transmit to them the progressive social and political views of the Popular Movement' (ibid.).

A member of the PB of the party acknowledged that the leadership was essentially trying to catch up with developments: 'This [mention of NGOs] was also the result of a reality: the members of the party who are members in such organisations because of a special interest and carry out activity [in them]' (interview, 11 May 2011, Nicosia). An overall lateness in the development of Cypriot civil society meant that NGOs (and more broadly CSOs without partisan affiliations) as political or social movements were indeed a phenomenon of the last decade (Taki & Officer 2008). Nonetheless, responding to the emergence of such organisations in an ad hoc manner is clearly a different action from taking the initiative to establish close and persistent links to them and the latter has been largely absent from AKEL's linkage strategy.

AKEL's relations with CSOs outside the Popular Movement have not exhibited any signs of strong or progressive organisational interconnection. They appear to be non-institutionalised to the degree that an established and organisationally embedded pattern of contact does not exist. No temporary or permanent committees linking AKEL and CSOs exist, no joint conferences are organised, there are no agreements about regular meetings, and manifesto drafting has never been the product of dialogue seminars or hearings. Rather, contact materialises ad hoc. Effectively it takes two forms: that of meetings between members of the leadership who are responsible for the party office under which the organisation's issues fall and the leading members of the organisation's AKEL-centred group, and that of invitations to party seminars and in some cases party congresses (see Allern 2010, table 12.1).

Direction of Influence in AKEL's Environmental Linkage

A number of indicators suggest that most influence lies with the party in what concerns its relations with both the Popular Movement and other CSOs. Congress decisions send the enduring message that the Popular Movement organisations are a central part of AKEL's modus operandi. Ideologically and at the level of the big decisions, the Popular Movement forms an extension of the party rather than a parallel cooperating force. The party is the central planner of the movement's political profile, its guide and its ultimate goal.

Evidence of this relationship between party and movement is that, on a number of high political issues, a decision has not been taken and announced by the Popular Movement organisations prior to the formalisation of the party's own stance. Indicatively, AKEL's decision for 'No' to the Annan Plan referendum[6] essentially bound EDON, PEO and POGO. These same organisations did not issue prior to the party any declarations on issues such as Cyprus's membership application to the EU in 1990, the European Constitution, the Lisbon Treaty and the economic policy measures of opposing governments. At election time all four of the Popular Movement organisations officially mobilise in favour of the AKEL ticket (or AKEL's favoured candidate in the case of presidential elections). Their members also generously contribute to the party's annual fundraising campaigns. However, the most illustrative example of the party's supremacy is perhaps the split of 1990. After they resigned or were removed from their senior AKEL offices, EDON and PEO officials were also expelled from their respective organisations.

Experience in government provides quite sharp examples of the Popular Movement's subordination to the party, especially within the context of the onset of the economic crisis and its effect on Cyprus. This impinges on the relations of three agents: the Christofias government, the party, and civil society organisations affiliated, or linked, to them. The AKEL-led government is bound by EU obligations to take measures and bring the economy in line with criteria set by Brussels. Some of the requirements conflict with AKEL's principles not to harm the rights and privileges of working people. In late 2011 AKEL Finance Minister Kikis Kazamias announced a number of economic measures, arguing that they were 'necessary [to avoid] the EU's Support Mechanism'. A few days later (on 19 November 2011) *Charavgi* (AKEL's newspaper) came out with the headline 'Salary Freeze in the Public Sector (for two years)', praising the measures and the minister's 'decisiveness', at a time when PEO was officially and forcefully against them (*Charavgi* 2011). Shortly thereafter, once the party's CC (including a substantial number of trade unionists) had voted unanimously in favour of the proposed government budget, which included a freeze in public sector salaries and other measures, PEO simply withdrew their previous (albeit unofficial) intention to call a strike and limited themselves to picketing, along with other trade unions. EDON was also initially positioned against some of the proposed measures, such as the decrease in the public sector's pay scales for new employees, but also silenced its opposition once AKEL endorsed the measure.

Trade unions have found themselves in conflict with their links to the party and/or the government, essentially because the shell of communist ideology is combined with what is essentially the pursuit of social democratic and liberal policies. The trade unions' will to defend their members' rights clash with decisions by the government and the party's support of these decisions in parliament. Although in certain cases these unions (essentially PEO) have tried to coordinate their efforts with the 'other' unions, there is an evident effort to keep some balance, which in the end benefits AKEL and the government. The party–government axis seems to be structured in such a way that reactions from within the Popular Movement against the AKEL-led government's decisions are effectively neutralised. With hindsight, the inclusion of leading figures from the Popular Movement within AKEL's leading bodies seems to be an important way of controlling these organisations, especially given the absence of precise ways through which the elements of the Popular Movement can collectively have direct input into party policy-making.

More broadly, AKEL's links with society were conceived and implemented from the outset in an instrumental way. Article 26 of the first constitution of the party in 1941 stated explicitly, 'In all extra-partisan, workers' and farmers' mass organisations, as well as in their leading bodies (trade unions, cooperatives, farmers' associations, associations of small shopkeepers, athletic unions, cultural clubs etc.), even in municipal councils and the parliament, if more than two members of the party participate, then they form a party group with the objective of reinforcing party policy within these organisations and bodies' (Papadimitris & Petrides 1980). The 1990 congress made explicit reference to the formation of party groups within professional, syndicalist and sports organisations—something that was repeated in the 1995 congress. Additionally, the party has been associated with a number of 'organisations inside organisations'. Prominent examples come from professional/syndicalist organisations: Προοδευτική Κίνηση Καθηγητών (Progressive Movement of High School Teachers) and Προοδευτική Κίνηση Δασκάλων (Progressive Movement of Primary School Teachers), which are, respectively, active inside Παγκύπρια

Οργάνωση Ελλήνων Διδασκάλων (Pan-Cyprian Organisation of Greek Teachers, POED) and Οργάνωση Ελλήνων Λειτουργών Μέσης Εκπαίδευσης (Organisation of Greek Functionaries of Secondary Education, OELMEK)—the main syndicalist organisations of teachers.

Arguably, the party's objective is not the loose participation of party members in these organisations but directed action that stems from the party's 'leading bodies at all levels' (AKEL 2010, p. 43) and secures the intervention and social capital formation in these organisations of the party as a political entity. In the case of the 2010 congress's reference to NGOs, AKEL essentially acknowledged the impossibility of establishing party groups within them. But the party was again the prime object of reference and the programmatic transfer and ideological transmission *towards*, and not *from*, NGOs was the declared objective.

Since 1990 a number of offices, each responsible for a specific policy area, were added to the party's structure. Among the duties of those responsible for each office—almost invariably members of the CC—is to maintain contacts with relevant CSOs (interview, 11 May 2011, Nicosia). By 2005 the party congress acknowledged the need for party groups in more and new fields (AKEL 2006, p. 57). In its Theses to the 2010 congress the CC also identified a link between specific (thematic) party offices and the formation of party groups in societal organisations: 'Where party offices are not established or weaknesses in their functioning present themselves, we do not manage to establish a party group' (AKEL 2010, p. 43). In other words, the party seems to want to strengthen party offices because it has observed that wherever there are such offices there are better chances of establishing a party group within the respective CSOs.

Programmatic influence running from CSOs (outside the Popular Movement) to the party is minimal in the formal sense, because a mechanism that binds the party to pledge exchanges is absent. The concerns of CSOs are incorporated into AKEL's manifestos at the discretion of the heads of each office, without procedures that secure CSOs' influence on the party. AKEL listens but avoids promises.

Factors Conditioning Linkage

Ideology

AKEL's priority is to establish relations with groups that fit the party's ideology and policy platform. AKEL's unaltered membership procedures accurately reflect the tradition of parties of the Third International type, where membership is restricted to those who are considered to have matured ideologically and who have satisfied the criteria of the party's screening mechanisms. The lack of formal ties between AKEL and CSOs is also indicative of a communist identity. Indeed, and above all, what becomes clear is the explicit and intentional approach of the party to either create its own ancillary organisations, whereby there is membership and leadership overlap, or 'infiltrate' new CSOs by forming party groups inside them. This seems to be part and parcel of the party's ideology, which sees the party leadership as the political and ideological guide for civil society and its organisations. This is so especially because those CSOs that lie beyond the Popular Movement are approached as capitalist products whose logic denies the class bases of society.

Electoral Competition

Electoral competition is important for the success of AKEL's linkage strategy. Unlike other European party systems, the Cypriot party system does not feature a large social democratic competitor, which means that social links on the left are dominated by AKEL. In addition, bipolarism is easily sustained due to the deep societal division between left and right, which extends to the economic sphere, encompassing businesses, production, consumption and financial relations. In this way, more modern channels of communication and influence are considered unnecessary for the party. That said, however, the party made openings to CSOs—in the congresses of 1986, 1990 and 2010—and democratised its internal procedures only after electoral challenges. In the first case the party polled the worst result in its history in the 1985 elections, and in the second case the threat of a splinter from the party (ADISOK) establishing itself as a firm competitor emerged, prompting the change to AKEL–Left-New Forces in order to get the message across that 'we are the new forces, not ADISOK'. Similarly, the opening up to NGOs in the 2010 congress can be explained by an electoral logic driven by the goal of pursuing more 'alternative' forms of societal penetration. AKEL realised the need to capitalise on the diversification of its members' social activities and project the image of a party in tune with social developments.

Party Leadership

The new leadership's decision to democratise internal processes followed almost five years of factional struggle—which resulted in a split and speculation about what would follow and how democratic the new AKEL would be in reality. Elsewhere it has been suggested that the above-mentioned organisational reforms of 1990 managed to portray a democratic image for the party, at a time 'when there was widespread belief in an anti-communist panacea' (Charalambous 2007, p. 441). However, organisational reforms also coincided with the election of a new party leader in 1988 (Christofias), who was internally challenged by opponents and thus had the urgent need to put in place his own team while avoiding giving the impression that an untouchable and unaccountable ruling circle was leading the party.

Party Model

Relations with the Popular Movement and the other organisational layers of the traditional subculture of the left mean that the party has never had to worry about membership levels and that a broad sphere of influence since the 1940s has rendered formal connections with other CSOs superfluous. Due to the presence, size and control by the party of these ancillary organisations, most of the organisational potential needed—in order to fund activities, initiate and sustain protest, disseminate educational and ideological messages, form a left-wing identity and win elections—has traditionally been done within the contours of the Popular Movement and is reinforced by partisan links to businesses. Therefore, if 'things get done' through the Popular Movement and other existing channels and practices, why engage in such relations with other CSOs which could potentially decrease the party's autonomy in determining policy and cause other problems? And why endanger the party's character by completely 'liberalising' member recruitment?

Additionally, the intense involvement of partisans in setting up CSOs and the penetration of the latter by party groups, or organisations closely connected to the party, reflect the vertically hierarchical and instrumentalist creation of linkage that has characterised many mass parties in Europe since the beginning of the century. Nevertheless, in the post-1990 period the party leadership has realised that the Popular Movement is not sufficient for the 'required' societal penetration. Thereafter, the mass party model, while continuing to benefit AKEL, has been complemented with new arrangements.

Conclusions

As an exceptional case of the European radical left—in terms of its electoral fortune and the employment of the mass model—AKEL has been much more comfortable than other parties in resisting drastic organisational change. While the party's most recent evolution vividly reflects a process of adaptation, neither its internal democratisation nor its strategic reorientation towards CSOs outside the Popular Movement has triggered the development of an alternative model of party organisation. Certainly, flexibility seems to have had a lot to do with AKEL's successful response to new developments, as expressed both in the internal reforms of 1990 and in more recent openings to CSOs.

AKEL did broaden its appeal, incorporate non-partisans in its ranks, give louder internal voice to its members and its supporters and respond in a timely and effective manner when new issues emerged and the relevance of new organisations came to the forefront of public debates. But, on both the participatory and environmental fronts, changes have been limited in extent. The leadership is still very strong because of its capacity to have the final say on almost all issues outside congress. Additionally, it can set the agenda and tone for those issues that are to be decided at congresses. The mass movement is still the party's child. Membership levels and activity do not exhibit any increase. And influence running from CSOs (including the Popular Movement) to the party appears to be very weak.

What is more, AKEL's taking on new issues did not have an effect on intra-party functioning, in the sense of substantially advancing participation or manifesting particular interest in articulating demands from civil society. Thus, no 'real' environmental linkage is taking place here. While AKEL has facilitated the emergence of a strong civil society in Cyprus, it also inhibits the latter's social and political effectiveness, in the classic liberal (and thus also non-strictly partisan) sense. Within the contours of Cypriot society, a smaller AKEL-centred society has been moulded into shape.

Finally, the logic of linkage in the case of AKEL is a product of complementary explanations. Our analysis agrees with Allern and Bale's (2012, p. 105) recent suggestion that future work 'should attempt to construct bridges between what are often "theoretical islands"'. All four factors that we identified at the beginning as potentially carrying some explanatory weight in conditioning linkage in the case of AKEL seem to matter, even if they do so against the background of the strong clientelistic and family-based practices of Cypriot society. Each factor explains some of the features of AKEL's participatory and environmental linkages with society in terms of intensity, institutionalisation and direction of influence. Concurrently, more than one of the factors set out above is often relevant to the explanation of each feature.

Acknowledgements

An earlier version of this article was presented at the 6th ECPR General Conference, University of Reykjavik. The authors extend their thanks to the participants in the panel 'Radical Left Parties and Civil Society in Southern Europe', the editors of this special issue, Antonis Ellinas and two anonymous referees for useful comments.

Notes

[1] See also what Sartori (2005, p. 20) calls the 'organisational mass party'.

[2] A third feature of AKEL is the presence of the Cyprus Problem as an issue of political competition in Cyprus, but this is something mainly related to the party's ideological trajectory and coalition strategy (Charalambous 2012).

[3] Especially the wide field of action available to the left, due to colonialism and the non-existence of organised politics or a party system.

[4] About 200 cooperatives operate in Cyprus, each with thousands of members. The movement's share of saving deposits was 40 per cent of the whole financial sector in 2007, which is indicative of its strength (see: http://www.cssda.gov.cy/cssda/cssda.nsf/All/C23193F14C74DA5CC2257386003D8B52?OpenDocument).

[5] In reality, AKEL's extensive links with the broader social body could not be reflected in the profile of its elected state officials, given that until the mid-1980s elected offices in the Republic of Cyprus were only 35 (MPs). This number increased after 1986 to more than 2,500 (local and other authorities) (Christophorou 2008, p. 92).

[6] In 2004 a referendum was carried out in Cyprus, about the Annan Plan—a plan to reunify the country, which has been divided since 1974. The majority of the Turkish Cypriot community voted in favour of the plan, while the majority of the Greek Cypriot community (including AKEL) rejected it.

References

AKEL (1986) Έκθεση Κεντρικής Επιτροπής προς το 16th Συνέδριο του ΑΚΕΛ [Report of the Central Committee to the 16th Congress of AKEL], Nicosia.

AKEL (1990) '17° Συνέδριο του ΑΚΕΛ: Υλικά και άλλα Ντοκουμέντα' [17th Congress of AKEL: materials and other documents], Nicosia.

AKEL (1991) 'Οι Υποψήφιοι Βουλευτές του ΑΚΕΛ για τις Βουλευτικές Εκλογές 1991' [AKEL's MP candidates for the parliamentary elections of 1991], Nicosia.

AKEL (1996) '18° Συνέδριο του *ΑΚΕΛ:* Υλικά και άλλα Ντοκουμέντα' [18th Congress of AKEL: materials and other documents], Nicosia.

AKEL (2001) 'Αποφάσεις και άλλα Ντοκουμέντα 19ου Συνεδρίου του ΑΚΕΛ' [Decisions and other documents of the 19th Congress of AKEL], Nicosia.

AKEL (2006) '20° Συνέδριο του ΑΚΕΛ: Αποφάσεις και άλλα Ντοκουμέντα' [20th Congress of AKEL: decisions and other documents], Nicosia.

AKEL (2010) 'Θέσεις της Κεντρικής Επιτροπής του ΑΚΕΛ για το 21ο Συνέδριο' [Theses of the Central Committee of AKEL for the 21st Congress], Nicosia.

AKEL (2011) 'Regulations for the functioning of AKEL', available online at: http://www.akel.org.cy/nqcontent.cfm?a_id=5294&tt = graphic&lang = 13, (accessed 10 July 2010).

Allern, E. (2010) *Political Parties and Interest Groups in Norway*, ECPR Press, Colchester.

Allern, E. H. & Bale, T. (2012) 'Conclusion: qualifying the common wisdom', *Party Politics*, vol. 18, no. 1, pp. 99–106.

Backes, U. & Moraeu, P. (2008) 'Conclusion', in *Communists and Post-communists in Europe*, eds U. Backes & P. Moraeu, Vandenhoeck & Ruprecht, Gottingen, pp. 535–608.

Bale, T. & Dunphy, R. (2007) 'Red flag still flying? Explaining AKEL – Cyprus's communist anomaly', *Party Politics*, vol. 13, no. 3, pp. 287–304.

Botella, J. & Ramiro, L. (eds) (2003) *The Crisis of Communism and Party Change: The Evolution of West European Communist and Post-Communist Parties*, Institut de Ciencies Politiques i Socials, Barcelona.

Charalambous, G. (2007) 'The strongest communists in Europe: accounting for AKEL's electoral success', *Journal of Communist Studies and Transition Politics*, vol. 23, no. 3, pp. 425–456.

Charalambous, G. (2009) 'The presidential elections of February 2009 in the Republic of Cyprus: the context, dynamics and outcome in perspective', *Cyprus Review*, vol. 21, no. 1, pp. 97–122.

Charalambous, G. (2012) 'Le parti progressiste du peuple travailleur (AKEL): un profil sociopolitique', in *Les Partis de la Gauche Anticapitaliste en Europe*, eds J. -M. De Waele & D. -L. Seiler, Economica, Paris, pp. 222–243.

Charavgi. (2011) 'Πάγωμα μισθών στο δημόσιο (για δύο χρόνια)' [Freeze of salaries in the public sector (for two years)], 19 November, p. 1.

Christophorou, C. (2006) 'Party change and development in Cyprus (1995–2005)', *South European Society and Politics*, vol. 11, no. 3, pp. 513–542.

Christophorou, C. (2008) 'The evolution of Greek Cypriot party politics', in *The Government and Politics of Cyprus*, eds H. Faustmann & J. Ker-Lindsay, Peter Lang, Oxford, pp. 83–106.

Hopkin, J. (2001) 'Bringing the members back in? Democratizing candidate selection in Britain and Spain', *Party Politics*, vol. 7, no. 3, pp. 343–361.

Ierodiakonou, L. (2003) *Τεθλασμένη Πορεία – Κύπρος 1959–2003, Πολιτικό Σύστημα, Πολιτικοί Θεσμοί, Διαδρομή Εκδημοκρατισμού* [A Zigzag Course – Cyprus 1959–2003, Political System, Political Institutions, Democratization Process], Alithia, Nicosia.

Katz, R. S. & Mair, P. (1995) 'Changing models of party organization and party democracy: the emergence of the cartel party', *Party Politics*, vol. 1, no. 1, pp. 5–28.

Kitschelt, H. (1994) *The Transformation of European Social Democracy*, Cambridge University Press, Cambridge.

Krouwel, A. (2006) 'Party models', in *Handbook of Party Politics*, eds R. Katz & W. Crotty, Sage, London, pp. 249–269.

Le Duc, L. (2001) 'Democratizing leadership selection', *Party Politics*, vol. 7, no. 3, pp. 323–341.

Panayiotou, A. (1999) 'Island radicals', PhD thesis, University of California, Santa Cruz.

Panebianco, A. (1988) *Political Parties: Organization and Power*, Cambridge University Press, Cambridge.

Papadimitris, P. & Petridis, P. (1980) *Ιστορική Εγκυκλοπαίδεια της Κύπρου, Τόμος 7* [Historical Encyclopedia of Cyprus, Volume 7], Nicosia Ekdoseis K. Epifaniou.

Peristianis, N. (2006) 'The rise of the left and the intra-ethnic cleavage', in *Britain in Cyprus: Colonialism and Post-colonialism 1878–2006*, eds H. Faustmann & N. Peristianis, Bibliopolis, Manheim, pp. 233–267.

Poguntke, T. (2006) 'Political parties and other organizations', in *Handbook of Party Politics*, eds R. Katz & W. Crotty, Sage, London, pp. 396–405.

Rawson, D. W. (1969) 'The life-span of labour parties', *Political Studies*, vol. 17, no. 3, pp. 313–333.

Sartori, G. (2005) 'Party types, organisation and functions', *West European Politics*, vol. 28, no. 1, pp. 5–32.

Scarrow, S., Webb, P. & Farrell, D. (2000) 'From social integration to electoral contestation: the changing distribution of power in political parties', in *Parties without Partisans: Political Change in Advanced Industrial Democracies*, eds R. Dalton & M. P. Wattenberg, Oxford University Press, Oxford, pp. 129–153.

Taki, Y. & Officer, D. (2008) 'Civil society and the public sphere', in *The Government and Politics of Cyprus*, eds H. Faustmann & J. Ker-Lindsay, Peter Lang, Oxford, pp. 205–230.

Van Biezen, I. (1998) 'Building party organizations and the relevance of past models: the communist and socialist parties in Spain and Portugal', *West European Politics*, vol. 21, no. 2, pp. 32–62.

Zorba, K. (2010) 'Πρώτος ήλθε ο Στέφανος' [Stephanos voted first], *Politis*, 29 November, p. 6.

Giorgos Charalambous (PhD Manchester) is currently an associate member of the teaching staff at the University of Cyprus and a visiting lecturer at Frederick University, Cyprus. His research and published work focus on the study of political parties (especially the European radical left), the domestic politics of European integration and Cypriot politics (parties, elections, institutions). His book titled *European Integration and the Communist Dilemma: Communist Party Responses to Europe in Greece, Cyprus and Italy* is forthcoming with Ashgate.

Christophoros Christophorou is Assistant Professor of Communications at the University of Nicosia. He studied education in Cyprus and Paris and political science in Athens and Lille. He participated in expert groups that drafted today's European media policies. He is the author of books and articles on elections, political parties, media and other subjects.

Index